This publication contains the opinions and ideas of its author. It is intended to provide helpful and informative material on the subjects addressed in the publication. The author and publisher specifically disclaim all responsibility for any liability, loss or risk, personal or otherwise, which is incurred as a consequence, directly or indirectly, of the use and application of any of the contents of this book.

WORKBOOK PRESS LLC
187 E Warm Springs Rd,
Suite B285, Las Vegas, NV 89119, USA

Website:	https://workbookpress.com/
Hotline:	1-888-818-4856
Email:	admin@workbookpress.com

Ordering Information:
Quantity sales. Special discounts are available on quantity purchases by corporations, associations, and others. For details, contact the publisher at the address above.

ISBN-13:	978-1-952754-01-2 (Paperback Version)
	978-1-952754-02-9 (Digital Version)

REV. DATE: 20/06/2020

BOOK #1

I Fought
Like a *Girl*
and I Won!

Nicole Alyse Dorman

**Illustrated By: Anastazija Bingham
("I Fought Like a Girl and I Won!")**

In loving memory of my grandmother Pauline Joyce Adams Baker 8/25/1926-
10/22/1974. She was 48 years old when she lost her battle with breast cancer. " I never
had the chance to meet you, but I love you and miss you so much!!!"
R.I.P

Thank-You to my mother Pamela and stepfather Wil, my remaining family and
extended family members for your support, love, and understanding!

Last, but definitely not least, Thank-You to my co-workers & parent friends at
Mountain View Elementary School in Harker Heights, TX. A million thank-you's cannot express my gratitude to all of you for being so supportive to my 3 children and I throughout my breast cancer journey!

CONTENTS

Preface 1

1. Who Am I? 4

2. Concerned About My Selfie!
(My Self-Exam, Not My IPhone Selfie.) 5

3. New Year, New Diagnosis! 8

4. The Game Plan: Tackling Breast Cancer 9

5. Meeting My Medical Team 12

6. Back To Work; Or Is It? 15

7. Positive Quotes To Give You Strength To Survive! 18

8. Breast Cancer Vocabulary 22

9. Raising BC Awareness Every Day!
Encouraging Women and Men To Get Yearly Mammograms! 29

10. Breast Cancer Resources 31

11. Eye Of The Tiger!
(Facebook Journal My Mother Created For Me.) 37

12. I've Got Some Mail! Sharing Some Cards and Letters from
My Family, Friends, and Co-workers 62

Preface

I Fought Like A Girl, And I Won!, is about my breast cancer journey from October 2013, until now. This is my first book, and I give it an "E" for everyone rating. Any Cancer diagnosis especially breast cancer affects everyone from children through adults.

I'm a single mother of 3 kids with a monthly income of $1,100. My income includes my part-time income with the Killeen Independent School District. I also am receiving child support for only one child. A huge curve ball was thrown at me when I received a phone call from my doctor telling me my needle core biopsy results. My doctor told me I had Invasive Ductal Carcinoma, a form of breast cancer!

My story reveals how I dealt with being told I was a statistic! The only difference was that I wasn't going down without a fight to survive! I discuss and educate readers about what I've endured throughout my journey. I share with readers how I told people about my diagnosis and how astonished I was for having so much love & support. I discuss and educate about my mastectomy and port-a-cath surgeries. I cut my hair very short before beginning chemotherapy in March 2014 to avoid in coming out in clumps.

My co-workers, parents, and friends at Mountain View Elementary were very envious (and still are) of me for returning to work with a smile on my face after every chemotherapy, and radiation treatments. When I was asked how I could keep smiling after everything I had been through, I simply replied that I was happy & grateful for having a second chance in life. I was blessed to be able to come to work after chemotherapy, most people have no energy and want to stay in bed to recover.

Any cancer diagnosis doesn't put life on hold. Monthly bills are still going to come in like clockwork. Children still need to go to school, and be cared for. I put everything in perspective once I was diagnosed, I didn't sweat the small things in life!

Once I was diagnosed, I became a survivor! I am sharing all of my experience that I had with breast cancer to educate, spread awareness, and to save someone else's life!

My book contains my entire journey, references, and the organizations that have assisted me with grants. While I'm constantly being told that I'm inspiring to many people, inspired myself to write this book! Everyone deserves a second chance in life, here is mine and I'm going to shine!

1. Who Am I?

Let me introduce myself before I began my story. I'm Nicole Alyse Dorman, born on January 15, 1979. I'm a single parent to three children; two boys 7&9, and a girl 15. I was born in Philadelphia, PA, I attended the Milton Hershey School in Hershey, PA from January 1989-June 2, 1996. I enlisted in the US Army on June 7, 1996. I had 8 weeks of basic training, and the 8 weeks of advanced individual training (AIT) to attend cooking school. I was in the Army Reserves for a year, while I attended East Stroudsburg University in East Stroudsburg, PA. I majored in Spanish Education, I wanted to become a Spanish teacher. In May 1997at the end of my first semester at ESU, I made the decision to join the Army full time and to be active duty. College life at ESU wasn't working out for me. I was fortunate to get orders for Dexheim Germany. I enjoyed my 3 year tour and did a lot of traveling in Europe when time allowed. I have been to Austria, Poland, Paris, Holland, and London. I have always enjoyed traveling, learning about different cultures, and lifestyles of people. I have been living in Killeen, Texas since February 2001. I had relocated to Killeen from Germany. I'm an honorably discharged Army Veteran, and am grateful for the awesome medical care I have received at the Temple VA Hospital. Cancer is a very expensive illness, I don't know what I would have done if I didn't have medical coverage through the Military VA. I currently am a crossing guard for the Killeen Independent School District (KISD). It is a part-time position where I work 20 hours a week. I love my job, and wouldn't trade it for the world! 😊

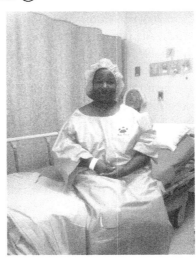

2. Concerned About My Selfie!
(My Self-Exam, Not My IPhone Selfie!)

In the middle of October 2013, I detected a painful lump in my right breast. I didn't think much of it but I wanted to get it looked at. I called the Women's Clinic at the Temple VA Hospital to make an appointment. The clerk on the phone whom I spoke with told me I could come in as soon as possible to do a walk-in mammogram. I was able to get a ride from a close friend of mine to the Women's Clinic on Wednesday November 27, 2013. When I went to check in with my Veterans I. D. card, I was told there were no walk-in mammograms! I explained to the clerk that I was told over the phone that I could come and do a walk-in and be seen today! There was no way I was going to go home without any answers! I had to be persistent but in a fashionable manner. My last plea to be seen was telling the clerk that my friend had taken time off from work to give me and my children a ride to Temple, TX from Killeen, TX (40 min drive). Moments later, a female nurse called me back to a room and asked me what my concern was. I told the nurse that I had complaints of a painful lump on my right breast that hurt all the time. I had a physical exam of both breast, and there was no doubt that the right breast was significantly swollen than the left! The nurse asked me what my pain level was, I wanted to say 100, but could only go as high as 10! The nurse told me that the lump was a "possible cyst". I didn't think the lump was a cyst because I didn't feel any fluid in it, only a hard mass. Obviously, I'm not a doctor, but I know my own body when something isn't right. The nurse said there was no reason to do a mammogram on me because I wasn't 40! Apparently, the fact that breast cancer is hereditary in my family didn't raise any red flags!!!!! My walk-in appointment was concluded by the nurse advising me to pick up a heating pad from the prosthetic department upstairs. The heat from the heating pad would alleviate the pain and discomfort I was having. I was also prescribed Naproxen 500mg for pain, and amoxicillin just in case the "possible cyst" was some king of infection. The nurse put in an order for an ultrasound to be done on me. The next 21/2 weeks went by as normal. I kept busy with work, and taking care of my children. I was taking the naproxen, and amoxicillin as prescribed, and also applying the heating pad throughout the day. The "possible cyst" was getting bigger, and more painful! It was the first week of December 2013 when I received a phone call from the Temple VA Women's Clinic. I finally had an appointment for December 18, 2013 for the ultrasound appointment!!! Unfortunately, I wasn't able to make that appointment, but I called to reschedule for a January 2, 2014 appointment.

Christmas, and New Year's 2014 went by faster than I could bat my eyelashes! At my appointment I was extremely scared, worried, and I had some anxiety about the ultrasound being done. I remember that I was talking along and being inquisitive! Who isn't when there is a procedure being done on them!? My eyes kept shifting from the screen to the technologists face. She looked very concerned, and I could tell something was wrong. I had asked her if everything was okay. She responded by saying, "the doctor will talk to you in a few minutes. He'll go over the results with you1" I thanked her and waited the few minutes for the doctor, but it seemed more like an hour! The doctor came in and introduced himself, he explained that the lump wasn't a cyst, but difficult to diagnose at that time. I also found out that I had a lot of calcification underneath my right breast. Calcification is the accumulation of calcium salts in a body tissue. It has nothing to do with the amount of calcium in your body! The doctor told me I was going to need to have a mammogram done, and a needle core biopsy. The doctor asked me if I was able to return on January 3, 2014 for the procedure. I told him that I wasn't able to return and asked if the biopsy could be done while I was already there at the Women's Clinic. I had the needle core biopsy performed on January 2, 2014, right after I had the bilateral (both breasts) mammogram done. The mammogram wasn't too bad, it was just painful because the lump on my right breast was being squished down! Ladies who have had mammograms done know what I'm talking about! =) The needle core biopsy on the other hand was very painful! I'm the type of person who doesn't flinch at the site of a needle; however having a long hollow needle entering a sensitive area was very unpleasant for me! This special needle had a trigger at the end of it to pull out breast tissue samples. When the doctor pulled the trigger it also made a loud noise. Normally 2-3 samples are collected but the doctor took 6 samples to be on the safe side. He didn't want me to have to come back to have another biopsy done if the samples weren't good enough. I had a liquid metal marker injected in my right breast so that when I had future mammograms, the doctor would know that I had tissue removed. Once the tissue samples were in the specimen cup I was allowed to see them, after all I was so involved with the procedure, asking every question in the book as to what was going on and what was happening next! The samples looked like silk worms in a clear liquid. The nurse told me that I would have my biopsy results in about 5 days. She gave me my brief after care instructions:

*No strenuous activities for a few days
*Take Naproxen 500mg for pain as needed

*Put the reusable gel pack in the freezer for cold compresses or in the microwave for hot compresses to help with the swelling

*Most importantly….Get plenty of rest; being a single mother of 3 kids gives me no time for any extra rest! (LOL) I had returned home around 4p.m.and at 6p.m., my 2 boys, my friend, and I were on our way to pick up my daughter from the Austin-Bergstrom Airport to pick up my daughter from spending the holidays with her dad. It was hard to tell my children that they couldn't give a big hug, and that mommy was in a lot of pain. When they asked why I was in pain, I could only tell them that I had a procedure done and that I had to take it easy for a few days to heal. I continued to pray about my biopsy results, hoping for the best. I was expecting a phone call on January 7, 2014 sometime with my results.

3. New Year, New Diagnosis

Tuesday January 7, 2014 had finally arrived. I had nervously called the VA Women's Clinic at noon to find out if my biopsy results were in. There were no results. At 3p.m. the nurse who originally seen me, and did the visual exam in November 2013, had called me to tell me my results. This was the phone call that would change my life forever. She nonchalantly said, "You have Invasive Ductal Carcinoma". I asked her to repeat what she said, I mean I heard her; I just wanted to hear the medical term again. I didn't know what the medical terminology meant. The nurse repeated" You have Invasive Ductal Carcinoma, a form of breast cancer!" Right then and there I just learned two things, 1. I had just been diagnosed with breast cancer, and 2. There was more than one form of breast cancer! At that very moment, my heart skipped a beat, I was in shock, and I started to feel sick to my stomach after hearing those two words **BREAST CANCER!** The nurse said that the good news was that breast cancer has a 95% survival rate if caught early. Being diagnosed with breast cancer was definitely not on my list of new years' resolutions! In the back of my mind, I was hoping that my results was a medical mix up. (Hey, these things happy all the time!) Wait! I remembered that at the beginning of the phone Call, I had to verify my name and social security number. I was still at work, on a break. I had to regain my composure to finish up my day before I could let the news sank in.

4. *The Game Plan;*
How I Would Tackle Breast Cancer.

The nurse said that I would be working with a team of specialists, and that I would have to make some crucial decisions. My VA medical team included my primary care doctor, oncologist, and surgeon. The nurse explained that I would definitely have to have surgery to get rid of most of the cancer. The surgery would be either a lumpectomy or a mastectomy, and my consultation with the surgeon would give me a better understanding of what would be better for me in my situation. The nurse concluded the phone conversation by saying, "Don't hesitate to call me in the next few days if you have any questions". I had a million questions...........I was scared and even worse I was thinking about how I was going to tell people about my new diagnosis. Any cancer diagnosis is not an easy subject to discuss. The news can, and will affect everyone differently. I had my list of people whom I wanted, and needed to tell but I wasn't sure about how to go about doing it. I have no problem talking to people, and being a social butterfly, but this was a brand new ball game! When you tell people your diagnosed with breast cancer, (or any other serious illness) you receive a more dramatic response, and you might have to repeat what you just announced! I decided to call my mother in Pennsylvania first, I was on a break at work, and wanted to tell her and my step-father Wil before I picked up my children from school. I was hoping to get their voice mail and leave a quick message saying, "Hi Mom, and Wil call me back when you have a moment to talk, I Love You!" Scratch that thought, my mom answered, and I had let her know I had just received my biopsy results. I asked her if she was sitting down, (Parent's you automatically know that when your child/ren ask you if you're sitting down, it's   BIG NEWS!) she said that she was. There was no beating around the bush, I told my mom straight out that I was diagnosed with Invasive Ductal Carcinoma, a form of breast cancer. I informed her that I would be seeing my primary care doctor, an oncologist, surgeon, and possibly other medical doctors. I told my mom that I would be updating her and Wil with news about my future appointments and updates as I received them. My phone conversation with my mom lasted roughly about 5-7 minutes. I had to get back to work, but I also know that she didn't want to stay on the phone too long with me. When I told my mom the news, I think she may have had flashbacks to when she was 14 in 1972 and her mother (my maternal grandmother) was diagnosed with breast cancer. I hadn't begun to play out in my mind how I was going to break the news to my children.

I spent a lot of time on the internet researching Invasive Ductal Carcinoma (IDC), and calcification I found out that Invasive Ductal Carcinoma starts in your breast ducts (no brainer there), and that 75%-80% of women have this type of breast cancer. Men can get breast cancer too, it's just not as common! The cancer can spread to other vital organs if not treated in time! I was getting worried because the only information I knew was that I had IDC. I didn't know how long I had this cancer in my body, what stage I was in, or how big the tumor was! I didn't know if I was going to live another year, or not. I was beginning to feel overwhelmed, but needed to calm down. I would soon find out the answers to all of my questions.

I contacted the American Cancer Society for support, and they sent me a "Welcome to Breast Cancer!" packet. The packet had a wealth of knowledge, and explained different services that the American Cancer Society offered. It was nice that they offered rides to my oncologist appoints at the Temple VA. I only used their pick-up service twice, but the volunteers that I had were really nice.

I had originally planned on waiting until I met my oncologist to sit down with my children and have "The Talk". I had read a section on the American Cancer Society on how to tell your children you have cancer. The site was extremely helpful and gave me guidance on how to tell my then 6, 8, and 14 year old children that I was sick. I didn't want to overload them with information that they wouldn't fully understand. I called my children in the den for a family meeting. There are some things in life that there are no right or wrong way to go about doing them. I looked in my children's eyes, and said "There's no easy way to say this, but mommy has breast cancer". My daughter who was 14 years old at the time had a better understanding of what I had just said. She took the news the hardest, and had run out of the room crying and screaming "Say it isn't true!" I told her to come back in the den because running away isn't going to make the cancer automatically disappear. I hugged all my kids tightly and told them that I love them so much. I explained that they cannot catch cancer from me, and that breast cancer wasn't a death sentence for me. I told them that my appearance was going to change, and I would need them to help more around the house. I told my kids that I would lose my hair when I had to do chemotherapy treatments, I might lose some weight, be more tired than usual. There is a long laundry list of breast cancer side effects, but I wanted to give them the short list, and not scare them. I kept calm, and remained strong while talking to them. I knew that if I broke down in tears while talking, my kids would cry too! Overall the discussion went better than I expected it to.

I found out a lot about my newly diagnosed illness;

1. A cancer diagnosis puts everything in a new perspective!

2. A cancer diagnosis doesn't stop the bills from coming in!

3. A cancer diagnosis lets you know who is really there for you!

5. *Meeting My Medical Team, & Surgery*

January 14, 2014 I had an appointment to meet my oncologist. I received more information and got the opportunity to ask some questions that have been swarming in my mind for a week. I must have had 1,000 questions! When it comes to your health there are no limits of how many questions you can ask! No one can rush you when you have an appointment either! As soon as introductions were made, my oncologist told me that I had to have a mastectomy. The size of my tumor and the amount of calcification underneath was too much to try to save. If I had a lumpectomy to get rid of the tumor, in time the calcification would have turned into cancer cells. I didn't want that, and I agreed to have the mastectomy performed. I asked my oncologist what stage, and grade my cancer was. She explained that information was unknown until I had surgery, and a pathology report was completed. Every cancer journey is different, some women can have chemotherapy treatments to shrink the tumor down, and then have a lumpectomy, followed by radiation treatments. For me my journey would start with a mastectomy, followed by chemotherapy, and possible radiation. Breast reconstruction would be delayed for 6 months to 1 year after my mastectomy. You know what? I was determined to do everything I could do in order to be her for my children, and loved ones!

January 15, 2014 was my 35th birthday. It was a great day overall. I was doing "Awesome" (no lie) for a woman who received a breast cancer diagnosis a week prior! I had begun to inform my coworkers at Mountain View Elementary about my health. Every time I told someone the news , it really dawned on me that I really did have cancer, Reality finally hit me! I wasn't in denial that I was sick, I still felt healthy and my normal self. I have never smoked cigarettes and I drink in moderation, so what gives?

On January 17, 2014 I had a consultation with the surgeon who was going to perform my mastectomy. I was the question queen again! This time I asked the anesthesiologist a lot of questions since I had no previous surgeries. I had never been put to sleep, and I wanted to make sure that I was going to be calm for the big procedure. I had put everything in God's hands, and prayed on my situation! My surgeon had set a January 28, 2014 date. I only had 11 days to prepare myself, and make arrangements for my children because I was going to be in the hospital overnight. I needed to have someone pick me up once I was discharged from the hospital. I had many appointments to go to before my surgery to make sure my body was healthy and strong enough to have the mastectomy. I had done a CAT scan, EKG, blood work, to name a few things. I also had blood drawn for the BRCA1 test to see if I carried the breast cancer gene. It took 4 weeks to get the results of that test, fortunately I am NOT a carrier! Many thanks goes out to my good friend (she knows who she is) for picking me up, and helping me out a lot! ☺

January 27, 2014 I had a visit from a co-worker (assistant principal) Mrs. T. She had come to the house leaving food, drinks, snacks for the kids, and I. Mrs. T told me that a bunch of the co- workers at Mountain View Elementary had donated money to purchase enough food for the next month. It was really nice that my co-workers have done that because it made things a little easier for me to recover from the surgery.

January 28, 2014 was here! There was no turning back, it literally was a do or die situation! My good friend took me to the Temple VA at 9:00 am. My surgery time was scheduled for 11:00 am. I had checked in, was explained the process of getting changed into my "gear", and waiting in the waiting area, and I was nervous as Hell! I was handed a blue buzzer (the kind you get when your waiting for your table at a restaurant). When the buzzer started blinking it was time for me to go back and get ready for show time! The surgery was a success and I had come into the recovery area at 3:30 pm. My friend who had driven me to the VA was extremely worried about me because no one had given her an update about me. My cousin Joyce who lives in the Austin area, had come to visit me once I was assigned a room upstairs. I hadn't seen my cousin since March 2010, so I was glad to see her briefly. Joyce had told me that my breast cancer diagnosis was a wake-up call for her to start getting yearly mammograms, and to keep in touch more often with family. I really had my mind set on going home the evening of my surgery, but I was told that I had to stay overnight for observations! Who was I kidding!? I did just have a major surgery! I was in a lot less pain than I had anticipated; morphine works wonders! ☺ It was difficult for me to look in the mirror, and look at my new battle scar. I had mixed emotions on how my life was going to be with my new image. I shouldn't have; after all I was alive! I was thinking about some what if questions: "What if I looked like a freak to other people?", and "What if I felt like I was less of a woman because of having the mastectomy?" I was even worried about how I would be treated when I would return to work how I would be treated. I know that everyone knew my situation and what I had just been through, but I was so worried about a lot of things. None of that should have mattered because I was determined to be a survivor! I was discharged from the Temple VA Hospital on January 29, 2014 and I was off work for 4 weeks. I was in pain for about 2 ½ weeks. I had 5 lymph nodes removed (axillary dissection) during the mastectomy, and the lymph nodes were tested to determine what stage I was in. It would take another 4 weeks to get my pathology report to find out the answer. I had to have 2 Jackson Pratt drains (J.P. drains) in my right side to drain fluids from my mastectomy. The drains were bigger than the drawings I had seen online; they looked like plastic grenades! I was instructed on how to empty them out and to create a vacuum so that the tubes could pull out the excess fluids. It was quite easy, and luckily I do not get squeamish at the site of blood. The only thing I didn't like about the drains is that they were stitched in to my side for 10 days! I felt like a marionette puppet with limited mobility! My discharge nurse advised me to get plenty of rest! "HA!" That was not going to be easy, especially with 3 children. There was housework that needed to be done, laundry, etc. Life doesn't stop when your diagnosed with breast cancer! I did get some rest in the mornings, but afternoons I did laundry, vacuumed, swept, and moped the floors. I didn't overdue anything because I was on a order of lifting no more than 10pounds for 6 weeks. I wanted to exercise and use my right arm as much as possible. I am at risk for lymph edema for the rest of my life, since I had the mastectomy. I just have to be careful to not cut my right hand, or arm. I can wear a compression sleeve at night if I want. I can't have my blood pressure taken on my right arm anymore, or any I.V.'s taken from my right arm. I have to be careful with what I do, being at risk for lymph edema is a bit scary, but it doesn't limit me from doing anything! When I was discharged from the Temple VA hospital I wasn't given any resources on where to seek any kind of assistance, I had to do my own research. I wasn't able to get a home health aide to help me at home because I wasn't old enough! If I had been a senior citizen who just had a mastectomy, then I would have qualified to have a nurse come to the house and help clean my surgery site, and change bandages, etc. I'm in no way complaining, I am very grateful that I was able to get good medical treatment at the Temple VA.

6. Back To Work; Or Is It?

The last week of February, I had called my boss to remind her that I was returning to work on March 3, 2014. She was glad to hear that I was healing well, and was returning back to work. I told her that I was ready to return back to work. I had also informed her that I would be starting chemotherapy sometime in March. When I told her that, she had told me how she was just recently informed that part-time employees for KISD are not qualified for the Family Leave Medical Act (FMLA) My disposition immediately went from happy to concerned; suddenly I wondered how receiving chemotherapy treatments would affect me, and my crossing guard job. My boss reminded me that I had already used all of my sick leave! I did have a lot of pre surgery appointments that were during my work hours. This news flash meant that depending on how I felt after my chemotherapy treatments, I may be fired from my job if I didn't come to work. That wasn't what I was expecting to hear, but that's life! I had read that many chemotherapy patients are really tired after a treatment, and are in bed for 1-2 days after treatment!!! Time would tell what was in store for me.

March 18, I had to have another surgery to have a medi-port put in my chest. I have small veins, and receiving chemotherapy every 2 weeks, would have me bruised worse than a peach! The surgery is normally a 20 minute procedure where the port and catheter tube are put in through your veins. My surgery went about an hour because of complications; I had to have the catheter fed through my jugular vein, which you can see sticking out of my neck. My neck and chest were painful for the first few days after surgery. My chemotherapy began on March 19, 2014 I started with 2 medicines at the same time. I had Adriamycin (red), and Cytoxen (clear). Adriamycin is the most toxic chemotherapy drug out there, with the most side effects. I was in chemotherapy for 2 ½ to 3 hours. I had my appointments scheduled at 11am so I had a lunch tray in the chemotherapy room. I didn't feel sick until the next day after chemotherapy. I felt nauseous, fatigued, and 2 days after chemotherapy I had to give myself a shot in the stomach. The shot is called Nuelasta and it helps to boost your white blood count. The Nuelasta shot had to be refrigerated until I self-administered it in my stomach. I had horrible bone pain within 24 hours after giving myself the shot, and it really hurt! The all over bone pain lasted about 2-3 days. I took Naproxen for pain. Remarkably, I always went to work the day after chemotherapy with a smile on my face! I count my blessings that I was able to get out of bed to come to work; I had to my job was on the line! It was not easy by a long shot, and I wasn't always feeling my best but it was doable.

As soon as I would feel better it was time for another chemotherapy treatment. I really didn't have time to rest and relax after my chemotherapy treatments. I had my children to take care of. In life we all have to make sacrifices in life. I had breast cancer but I wasn't going to use that as a crutch and be lazy. I also was not going to sit in a corner and feel bad for myself because I had this illness. I was going to stay positive, and had my mind set to beat breast cancer! Every chemotherapy treatment I had my blood drawn from my medi-port for my lab work. The labs were necessary for my oncologist to monitor my blood counts, etc.

In April, 2014 I was fitted for a mastectomy bra, and a breast prosthesis. I was almost 4 months post surgery and I finally had a sense of balance. I felt normal and looked normal! I was very pleased with my prosthetic, and bra's. Not everyone handles a breast cancer diagnosis the same, and not every experience is the same. It was easy for me to remain positive, and to be hopeful that I was going to win the fight. I wanted to be another statistic… ….a survivor statistic! I had the attitude that I was going to beat breast cancer; I was determined that it wasn't my time to leave yet! You may not realize that when you smile at someone, you may make someone's day! A smile goes a long way, you never know until you smile at someone or receive a smile back.

July 30, 2014 through September 10, 2014 I underwent 30 treatments of radiation at the Killeen Cancer Center. I had the most awesome, upbeat, professional radiology staff I've ever met! I went to my appointments Monday-Friday at 9:30 am. I felt that radiation was a slice of pie, compared to the chemotherapy treatments I endured every 2 weeks for 4 months! I had very few side effects which included fatigue, darkening of my skin at the treatment sites, and skin tenderness. The final 2 weeks of my radiation was the most painful for me. My skin had started to peel under my right arm pit and around my mastectomy site. There was a foul odor (which I was told was normal), and I had swelling everywhere I was peeling. I had pain that wouldn't quit! I was prescribed pain medicine which I only took at night so I could go to sleep. During the day I had tolerated the pain while I was at work. Even though I've complete all of my radiation, my radiology oncologist wants me to do follow up appointments every few months with me to make sure my skin is healing properly.

I am fortunate that I caught my breast cancer early on! I had endure a lot through my journey, but my friends, family, faith, hope, courage, and my positive attitude helped me win my battle. I have been taking Tamoxifen since September. I have to take this pill once a day for 5 years. I will be having reconstruction surgery in the Spring of 2015.

7. Poems And Quotes To Inspire You Every Day!

What Cancer Cannot Do
Cancer Is So Limited……..
It cannot cripple love
It cannot shatter hope
It cannot corrode faith
It cannot destroy peace
It cannot kill friendship
It cannot suppress memories
It cannot silence courage
It cannot conquer the spirit
It cannot steal eternal life
"The Senior Times", Montreal

"LIFE is not about waiting for the storm to pass, it's about learning to DANCE in the RAIN."-unknown

"Someone once asked me how I hold my head up so high after all I've been through. I said, it's because no matter what, I am a survivor. Not a victim."-Patricia Buckley

"My strength didn't come from lifting weights. My strength came from lifting myself up every time I was knocked down." - unknown

"I admire people who choose to shine even after all the storms they've been through." - unknown

"Sometimes things happen to us that we just don't understand. Those things sometimes become the doors and windows to our destiny." - Andrea Nugent

"Never, Never be afraid to do what's right, especially if the well-being of a person or animal is at stake. Society's punishments are small compared to the wounds we inflict on our soul when we look the other way." - Martin Luther King Jr.

"The trouble with not having a goal is that you can spend your life running up and down the field and never score." - Bill Copeland
"It's never too late to be what you might have been."- George Eliot

"If opportunity doesn't knock, build a door." –Milton Berle

"I haven't failed. I've just found 10,000 ways that won't work." – Thomas Edison

"When you come to the end of your rope, tie a knot and hang on."- Franklin D. Roosevelt

"In between goals is a thing called life, that has to be lived and enjoyed." – Sid Caesar

"The man who removes a mountain begins by carrying away small stones." – Chinese Proverb

"The difference between ordinary and extraordinary is that little extra." – Jimmy Johnson

"When I hear somebody sigh, "Life is hard," I am always tempted to ask, "Compared to what?" – Sydney Harris

"Do not let what you cannot do interfere with what you can do."- John Wooden

"Don't let life discourage you; everyone who go where he is had to begin where he was."- Richard L. Evans

"If you want to make your dreams come true, the first thing you have to do is wake up."- J.M. Power

"Life is 10% what happens to us and 90% how we react to it."- Dennis P. Kimbro

"A successful man is one who can lay a firm foundation with the bricks that others throw at him." – Sidney Greenberg

"People often say that motivation doesn't last. Well, neither does bathing- that's why we recommend it daily."- Zig Ziglar

"The man who has confidence in himself gains the confidence of others." – Hasidic Proverb

"Do not go where the path may lead, go instead where there is no path and leave a trail." – Ralph Waldo Emerson

"Enjoy the little things, for one day you may look back and realize they were the big things."- Robert Brault

"Be who you are and say what you feel, because those who mind don't matter and those who matter don't mind."- Dr. Seuss

"Not everything that can be counted counts, and not everything that counts can be counted." –Albert Einstein

"By failing to prepare, you are preparing to fail."- Benjamin Franklin
"The pessimist sees difficulty in every opportunity. The optimist sees the opportunity in every difficulty."- Winston Churchill

"The journey of a thousand miles begins with the first step."- Lao Tzu

"Feed your faith and your fears will starve to death."- Author Unknown

"Attitude is a little thing that makes a big difference." - Winston Churchill

"The human spirit is stronger than anything that can happen to it.: -C.C. Scott
Pink Ribbon Poem
"Tune In" to good health
A Pink Ribbon you'll see
It stands for awareness
For the whole world to see.
"Tune IN" to good health
Have a mammogram each year
Do self-breast exams
And you'll have nothing to fear.
"Tune In" to good health
And quick as a wink
With early detection
You'll be in the Pink.
By: Linda Hotger
Cancer Is A Bridge To Pass
Cancer is A Bridge to Pass is Just Another Obstacle
Cancer is a bridge, that some have to pass. Some go

all the way across, but some fall along the way.
It's tragic those who fall, when they have come so far.
They fought such a courageous battle, but the war has been won.
They fell off.
Some make it across. They are the lucky ones. The ones who fight so hard
and never give up. They make it across. They win the fight.
They wind the battle.
They win the war. Cancer is just an obstacle.
We all have to stick together to pass it.
If we can find a cure, millions of lives will be saved.
Humankind will be able to find a cure
with the right funding. Help me fight cancer.
Help my friends, their families and my family.
Help fight cancer. You will be rewarded.

By: Mike Becker

"We cannot direct the wind but we can adjust the sails." – Author Unknown
"A cloudy day is no match for a sunny disposition." – William Arthur Ward

8. My Breast Cancer Vocabulary Chapter

The following vocabulary words are everything that I went through during my journey and have yet to experience! I've created this vocabulary so everyone can understand the definitions!

A

Adjuvant Treatment - therapy offered in addition to an initial surgical procedure to decrease the risk of relapse. Fact: I underwent chemotherapy, radiation, and currently am going through hormonal therapy. I am prescribed 20 mg of Tamoxifen daily for the next five years.

Alopecia - a condition that causes the loss of hair from anywhere on your body, mainly the scalp. Fact: I cut my hair short before I started chemotherapy. I knew that the first two chemotherapy medicines I was taken would cause hair loss. I didn't want my hair falling out in clumps! When my hair did fall out, my scalp was extremely tender, and sore!

Analgesic - any drug that is prescribed or administered to take away pain without the loss of consciousness by blocking messages transferred between the brain and pain receptor site. Fact: Morphine is a analgesic. I had morphine administered through my IV after I had my right mastectomy. Hydrocodone is another analgesic. I was prescribed this and only took it at night because of the side effects, not to mention it is a narcotic! I had also took hydrocodone when I was peeling and had painful radiation burns!

Antiemetic - a drug taken to alleviate nausea, and vomiting. Fact: I was prescribed medicine to help me not feel nauseated after each chemotherapy round.

Axillary Dissection (Lymph Node) - the surgical removal of lymph nodes located in the armpit area. Fact: during my mastectomy, I had 5 lymph nodes removed. My biopsy results revealed that 1out of 5 removed lymph nodes contained cancer cells.

B

Biopsy - the removal and microscopic analysis of a small piece of live tissues performed to determine an accurate diagnosis. Fact: I had a needle core biopsy in December 2013, and the results told me that my cancer was 2.2cm x 2.5 cm (2in x 2.5 in).

Bone Scan - a medical procedure that involves a radioactive substance (tracer) injected into a vein. The tracer travels from the bloodstream to the bones allowing for a scanner to photograph the condition of the bones. Fact: I had to do a bone scan in January 2014 before having the surgery.

BRCA1 - A tumor suppressor gene embedded without the instructions to produce a protein that helps maintain a healthy cell division and growth as well as repair damaged DNA if possible and destroy if unable to repair. BRCA1 derives its name from being the first discovered hereditary gene mutation associated with a higher risk of developing breast cancer. Fact: I had blood drawn to be tested and sent to a lab to see if I carried the BRCA1 gene. Fortunately, the test results came back negative.

Breast Cancer - the development of malignant (cancerous) cells that originate in the tissues of the breast, usually the duct and lobules. Fact: I had Invasive Ductal Carcinoma.

Breast Implant - a prosthetic device consisting of a silicone outer shell and filled with a silicone gel or saline (salt water) that is implanted to augment, reconstruct, or create the physical form of female breasts. Fact: One of my reconstruction options is to have a breast implant.

C

Cancer - term used to describe nearly 1—disease characterized by a malignant and invasive tumor caused by the uncontrolled division and growth of abnormal cells. Fact: I had breast cancer!

Cancer Cell - abnormal cell that divides and reproduces with uncontrolled growth, becoming part of a malignant tumor when conjoined with other like cells. Fact: I had 5 lymph nodes that contained cancer cells.

Carcinoma - referring to any cancer that initially develops in the skin or other tissues, including breast tissue. Fact: I had Invasive Ductal Carcinoma.

Cat Scan (Computer Axial Tomography, Computed Tomography, CT Scan) - a cross sectional image of the body produced by using x-ray technology that may include the liver, blood vessels, organs, or soft tissue. Fact: I had to have a CT Scan before I had my mastectomy in January 2014.

Chemotherapy - treatment of cancer that uses chemotherapeutic agents that are selectively destructive and toxic to malignant cells and tissue. Fact: I had 4 months of chemotherapy. I took a total of 3 chemotherapy drugs Adriamycin, Cytoxan, and Taxol. I went every 2 weeks for my treatments.

Chronic - used to describe a disease or health condition that has a long duration (more than 3 months or recurs frequently). Fact: my breast cancer lasted more than 3 months. I had found the lump in October 2013, but was diagnosed in January 2014.

Core Biopsy - diagnostic medical procedure in which a thin hollow needle is inserted into the lump or mass. The doctor may obtain a more accurate diagnosis by examining the tissue sample under a microscope. Fact: I had a core needle biopsy performed on January 2, 2014. I had 6 samples extracted from the tumor.

E

Estrogen - a group of compounds of hormones produced primarily by the ovaries that are responsible for menstrual cyclical changes, and for the development and maintenance of secondary sex characteristics.

Estrogen Receptor(ER) - refers to a protein receptor found within cells that once activated by the hormone estrogen, allows the estrogen to bind to DNA which may cause the cell to grow. Fact: my breast cancer was caused from estrogen receptors.

H

Her 2/Neu (Human Epidermal Growth Factor Receptor 2) - refers to a gene that is responsible for sending signals to the cells with instructions to divide, grow, or repair. A mutation (Her 2 Positive) only occurs in certain cancer cells, which promotes the division and growth of the cells. An Her2 mutation is not hereditary. 15%-20% of all breast cancers are Her 2/Neu –positive.

I

Invasive Carcinoma - refers to cancer cells that penetrate the basement membrane which allows the cells to invade, or spread to the surrounding healthy tissue.

L

Lymph edema - refers to localized fluid retention or swelling (usually in an arm or leg) due to an obstruction in the lymphatic system damage to or removal of lymph nodes can cause lymph-edema Fact: I'm at risk for lymph edema in my right arm due to having 5 lymph nodes removed. I can't have any blood draws or blood pressure taken on my right arm. I also have to be careful to not cut my right hand or right arm.

Lymph Nodes - round or oval shaped structures distributed throughout the body, including the armpits and stomach. These structures act as filters for harmful substances and contain cells that attack germs and help fight infection. Fact: I had five lymph nodes removed when I had my mastectomy. My pathology report found that the breast cancer was trying to spread to other organs in my body.

M

M. Malignant Tumor - a cancerous mass of tissue that has no physiological purpose other than to survive and grow. Fact: I had a malignant tumor that I detected on my right breast in October 2013. I grew more concerned when the tumor got bigger!

Mammogram - refers to a medical procedure that produces an x-ray image of the breast. Mammograms are used by doctors to detect any abnormalities such as tumors. Fact: My doctor refused to give me a mammogram in November 2013 because I wasn't 40! I asked for another opinion especially since I have a family history of breast cancer.

Mastectomy - the surgical removal of all or part of one or both breasts.. Fact: I had a simple mastectomy where all the tissue, breast, and nipple was removed! The that it was my first surgery and it was considered major surgery was pretty scary! I came through with flying colors!

O

Oncologist - a doctor who specializes in the diagnosis, study, and treatment of neoplastic diseases particularly cancer. Fact: My oncologist is very understanding and a patient doctor! (no pun intended!) My first meeting with her was on January 14, 2014. Although I'm in remission now, I still see her every month and I have to do labs through my medi-port.

P

Pathology - the scientific study of the nature of diseases, with an emphasis on the structural and functional changes in bodily tissue as a disease progresses. Fact: my pathology report gave me a breakdown on what was found in my breast tissue that was removed when I had the mastectomy.

Prosthesis - an artificial device used to augment or replace an impaired or missing body part. Fact: in April 2014, I was fitted for 3 mastectomy bras and a breast prosthetic. I was amazed at how realistic the prosthesis was! Wearing the prosthetic gives me a sense of balance (no pun intended, or was it?!) It also gives me confidence that I don't have when I'm not wearing it. It is a temporary fix until I have my reconstruction surgery in the spring of 2015.

R

Radiation Oncologist - a doctor who specializes in overseeing the use of radiation therapy as a treatment method for patients with cancer. Fact: I first met my radiation oncologist in June 2014 for a consultation. My doctor had explained that I needed 30 treatments of radiation therapy. Reconstructive Surgery- type of surgery performed to replace the breast and the skin of a breast that was previously removed with the goal of restoring symmetry between the two breast. Fact: my skin has to heal for 6 months after my last radiation treatment. My last radiation treatment was September 10, 2014.

Remission - refers to the period when a disease appears to be inactive. A complete remission indicates no sign of the disease. Partial remission indicates that there is a significant decrease in the number of decreased cells and a few symptoms remain. Fact: I have been in remission since July 10, 2014! I had a CT Scan done on July 7, 2014 and the results came back..........NO CANCER CELLS IN MY BODY! God Is Good.......All The Time!☺

T

Tamoxifen - an anti-estrogen commonly used in hormone treatment therapy due to its ability to block the actions of the female hormone estrogen. Fact: I started taking Tamoxifen on September 29, 2014. May 2014- September 29, 2014 I had a nice long break from my menstrual cycle. It returned after taking one 20 mg pill of Tamoxifen! What happened was that my last round of chemotherapy Taxol had put my body in a pre-menopausal state. I have to take Tamoxifen daily for the next 5 years!

Tram Flap - surgical procedure that used the transverse rectus abdominis myocutaneous (TRAM) flap to carry lower abdominal fat muscle, and skin to the breast in reconstructive surgery as an alternative to a prosthesis. Fact: my reconstruction surgery will done using the TRAM Flap procedure. It is a transport surgery, which means the surgeons have to make sure that tissues and blood flow are correct. It's an extensive 8-10 hour surgery with a minimum of 4 days in the hospital.

U

Ultrasound Examination - a noninvasive painless imaging method that uses high frequency sound waves to produce fairly precise images of the body's organs and structures. It is used by doctors to diagnose and treat a variety of medical conditions. Fact: my ultrasound I had performed in December 2013 revealed unsettling images. The doctor decided to do the mammogram and needle core biopsy.

9. Raising BC Awareness Every Day! Encouraging Women and Men To Get Yearly Mammograms!

The purpose of my book "I Fought Like A Girl, And I Won!", is to share my story. Every breast cancer survivor story is different, unique, and important.

I cannot say enough times how important it is as a woman to do monthly self-exams! Don't wait to get a detected lump examined by your doctor. It's better to be safe than sorry is an understatement, more importantly if you have a family history of breast cancer, you need to be checked. If your under 40, and your told that your too young to get a mammogram, then you need and have to the right to get a second opinion! Don't take "No" for an answer when it comes to your health. It's 2015 now, and women are being diagnosed with breast cancer in their 20's!

We've all heard it before........Early detection is best, and that is the truth! I was fortunate that I found the lump early before it spread to my other organs. Woman who are diagnosed early with breast cancer have about a 95% survival rate. Life really is too short, so don't gamble with your chances of surviving if you find a lump. A breast cancer scare is very scary, but for most women a lump is benign.

I have been in remission since 7/10/2014, which coincidentally is my diagnosis date flipped 1/07/2014! I had a CAT Scan performed on July 3, to verify that there were no more cancer cells in my body! Peace of mind is what I wanted and needed after my ordeal I have been through! I continue to see my oncologist, and my radiologist physicians every 3 months for check ups and labs. I am over joyous to have been blessed with a second chance in life! There are too many other women who have lost their battles with breast cancer. I want to Remarkably, I always went to work the day after chemotherapy with a smile on my face! I count my blessings that I was able to get out of bed to come raise breast cancer awareness everyday, not just in the month of October. I inspired myself and had the self-motivation to write this book tell my story to help spread breast cancer awareness worldwide!

Thank-you for purchasing and reading my story!

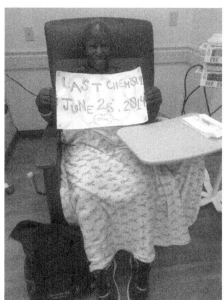

10. Breast Cancer Resources

A breast cancer diagnosis is very stressful, and a hard pill to swallow! There are mixed emotions from everyone you tell the news to, and you will feel overwhelmed like there is no where to go for help. There is help out there for financial, cleaning, prescriptions and other expenses you just have to know where to find it. The internet is a wealth of knowledge, and a very powerful tool! This resource guide is to let you know that you're not alone in your journey!

- Academy of Nutrition and Dietetics www.eatright.org
- Adjuvant www.adjuvantonline.com
- American Cancer Society www.cancer.org
- American College of Radiology www.acr.org
- American Institute for Cancer Research www.aicr.org
- American Medical Association www.ama-assn.org
- American Psycho social Oncology Society www.apos-society.org/ survivors/helpline/helpline.aspx
- American Society of Plastic Surgeons www.plasticsurgery.org/ reconstructive-proceedures/breast-reconstructions
- Angel Flight www.angelflight.com
- Army of Women www.armyofwomen.org
- Break Away From Cancer www.breakawayfromcancer.com/ breastcancer.org
- Breast Cancer Freebies www.breastcancerfreebies.com
- Cancer care www.cancercare.org
- Cancer Net www.cancer.net
- Cancer Support Community www.cancersupportcommunity.org
- Cancer Treatment Centers of America www.cancercenter.com
- Caring Bridge www.caringbridge.org
- Cleaning For A Reason www.cleaningforareason.com
- Chemo Angels www.chemoangels.wix.com
- Dream Foundation www.dreamfoundation.org
- Dr. Susan Love Research Foundation www.drsusanloveresearchfoundation.com
- Fertile Hope www.fertilehope.org
- FORCE (Facing Our Risk Of Cancer Empowered) www.facingourrisk.org

- Foundation for Women's Cancer www.foundationforwomenscancer.org
- Hope for Two" The Pregnant with Cancer Network www.pregnantwithcancer.org
- Imerman Angels www.imermanangels.org
- Inflammatory Breast Cancer (IBC) Research Foundation www.ibcresearch.org
- Live strong Foundation www.livestrong.org
- Living Beyond Breast Cancer www.lbbc.org
- Locks of Love www.locksof love.org
- Look Good Feel Better www.loogoodfeelbetter.org
- MD Anderson Cancer Center www.mdanderson.org
- Medscape www.medscape.com
- Metastatic Breast Cancer Network (MBCN) www.bbcn.org
- National Breast Cancer Coalition www.breastcancerdeadline2020.0rg
- National Cancer Institute www.cancer.gov
- National Center for Complementary and Alternative Medicine (NCCAM) www.nccam.nih.gov
- National Coalition for Cancer Survivor ship (NCCS) www.canceradvocacy.org
- National Comprehensive Cancer Network www.nccn.com
- National Hospice and Palliative Care Organization www.nhpco.org
- National Institutes of Health www.nih.gov
- National Lymph edema Network (NLN) www.lymphnet.org
- National Society of Genetic Counselors www.nsgc.org
- NC1-Designated Cancer Centers www.cancer.gov/researchfunding/extramural/cancercenters/find-a-cancer-center
- Office of Cancer Complementary and Alternative Medicine (OCCAM) www.cam.center.gov
- Prevent Cancer Foundation Co-Pay Relief www.preventcancer.org
- Reach to Recovery Program www.cancer.org/treatment/supportprogramservices/reach-to-recovery
- Sisters Network, Inc. www.sistersnetworkinc.org
- Stand Up To Cancer (SU2C) www.standup2cancer.org
- Susan G. Komen Breast Cancer Foundation www.komen.org
- Triple Negative Breast Cancer (TNBC) Foundation, Inc. www.tribcfoundation.org
- U.S. Food and Drug Administration www.fda.gov
- Young Survival Coalition www.youngsurvival.org

LINDA M. KERR
P O BOX 474
2181 LAKESIDE DRIVE
TOBYHANNA, PENNSYLVANIA
18466-0474

29 JUL 14

Dear Ma'am:

I write this letter of reference on behalf of Ms. Nicole Dorman, or Nikki, as she is known to me. I have the incredible honor of knowing Nikki for almost 20 years now. Her Mother and Stepfather were stationed at Tobyhanna Army Depot, where I worked in youth programming. Over the years, I have watched Nikki grow and become a beautiful woman and loving mother. Her life's journey has not been traveled without many challenges. She is a single parent, raising three beautiful, intelligent and compassionate children. Nikki is a United States Army Veteran. She is currently employed by a school district; however it is a part-time job. Her income is very limited and she does not receive support from two of the children's Father.

Most recently, as a matter of fact one week before her birthday in January (2014), Nikki was diagnosed with breast cancer. That is a scary diagnosis for anyone, but to get that diagnosis and know that you are the sole provider for three minor children must have been all the more devastating. Nikki had a mastectomy and then endured four months of chemotherapy. All the while smiling, maintaining a positive attitude and taking care of her three beautiful children; making sure their needs were met and fighting for her life. As of today, Nikki will undergo six weeks of radiation treatment: every day for six weeks! She continues to be determined to beat cancer and win this battle.

Never once have I heard Nikki say, "Why me" or "I can't do this." Her determination, faith in God and commitment to her children are what keep her going and keep her saying, "I will beat this," "I am a survivor!" She quite frankly is an amazing woman: one that I revere and admire beyond words. We all know that nothing in life is guaranteed, but I can say with absolute guarantee, I have never met anyone in my lifetime with more determination than Nicole Dorman: and while it may sound cliché, Nikki truly exemplifies the lyrics of The Eye of the Tiger. She is determined to rise above. She is a survivor and I know that with your help, she can continue to rise above and make a difference in the lives of all who have the honor of knowing her.

Thank you for considering Nikki as a recipient of assistance from your wonderful organization. Should you have any questions for me regarding this reference, please feel free to contact me at (570) 656-8326.

Respectfully,

Linda M. Kerr

MOUNTAIN VIEW ELEMENTARY SCHOOL
500 Mountain Lion Rd
Attention: (254) 336-7900
Harker Heights, Texas 76548

Dr. Randy Podhaski   *Dona Thompson & Grace Ashworth*
Principal   Assistant Principals

Every Child, Every Day, Every Where...
No Matter What!

August 14, 2014

To Whom it May Concern,
I am happily writing a letter on behalf of Nikki Dorman.
I have known her for over a year and have known her to be an extremely hard worker. She is always looking for things to do so that she can help out where needed. She does this with such a pleasant attitude and she is always cheerful.

She has had a lot on her plate this past year. She not only is a single parent of three, but then she got the devastating cancer diagnosis. Having breast cancer, going through a mastectomy, 4 months of chemotherapy, and now 6 weeks of radiation, along with being a single parent of 3 children on a limited income of $1,000, didn't stop her from being a great parent and a appreciative employee. She is truly a treasure and deserving of any assistance that you could give her.

If you have any questions, please don't hesitate to call me.

Dona Thompson
Dona Thompson

Memorandum

To:	Nicole Dorman
From:	Heidi Smotherman, Lead Crossing Guard
C. C.	John Dye, Director of Safety
Re:	Appreciation Letter

On Thursday, May 29, the Safety Office sent us an e-mail concerning the "Crossing Guard" at Mountain View, on Wampum and Mt. Lion. Attached is the email.

I just want to say that very few crossing guards get accolades from passing motorists. The fact that you got such an accolade speaks very highly of your attitude, friendliness, and willingness, to be on your corner, in all kinds of weather.

I want to say, Thank you very much, not only for doing a wonderful job, but doing it cheerfully.

You are a credit to the Crossing Guards, Mountain View, and KISD. Keep up the good work.

You are appreciated!!!

Smotherman, Heidi

From:	Dye, John
Sent:	Thursday, May 29, 2014 8:35 AM
To:	Smotherman, Heidi
Subject:	FW: crossing guard

We rarely get good reports.

-----Original Message-----
From: Bradley, Megan
Sent: Thursday, May 29, 2014 8:08 AM
To: Dye, John
Subject: crossing guard

I wanted to take time, before the year ends and I forget, to tell you how friendly one of your crossing guards is. She is at the corner of Wampum and Mountain Lion near Mountain View and Union Grove each morning. She waves to all of the cars as they come through with a big smile on her face (even when it is cold or rainy) and the walkers all seem to chat with her. She helps take the "drab" out of going to school in the morning!

Megan Bradley
Chief Financial Officer
Killeen Independent School District
(254)336-0157

1

11. Eye Of The Tiger- Nikki's fight
(FB Journal My Mom Created For Me Please Check
Out The Page on FB)

January 7, 2014
(Mom) A week before Nikki's 35th birthday; test results of her biopsy show she has a form of breast cancer. We are using this group page for support and to keep family and friends updated on her progress. Nikki is in good spirits and will get more information from her doctors next week... And the journey begins. Thank-you for being with us all throughout this journey.

January 10, 2014
Good Morning Everyone! Words cannot express how blessed, and thankful I am to have such a great support group. I will updates when I have appointments, etc. I am in good spirits and am feeling GREAT today!!

January 13, 2014
Happy Monday Everyone! I hope that you all had a great weekend! My weekend was great. Anastazija, Marcos, and Caesar stayed at a friend's house Saturday. I went and did some grocery shopping at HEB, Walmart, and enjoyed dinner at Applebee's Saturday evening! Sunday was more of a relaxed day where I ironed my clothes, and the kids' clothes for this week. I was going to wait until Tuesday night (January 14) to tell the kids about my cancer diagnosis, but I didn't want to overload them with information. Annie took the news the hardest being the oldest at 14. Caesar and Marcos were too young at 6 and 8 years to understand the reality of what I just told them. I assured them that my illness wasn't their fault and that I love them very much!

January 14, 2014
Hi Everyone! Here is my latest update: I met with my oncologist Dr. Dodlapati. She allowed me to look over my biopsy and ultrasound results while she translated to me what everything meant. At this time, she doesn't know what stage I'm at because a lymph node has to be taken out during surgery and tested. The mass is 2.5 cmx2 cm (over 1 inch long and 1 inch wide) I am at grade 1 which is good, meaning it doesn't look like the cancer cells have spread beyond my right breast. I do have a lot of calcification (cancer cells that are old but not invasive). Dr. D says that my short term plan is surgery; have a lumpectomy followed by radiation , or mastectomy. I will

find out more about that when I meet with the surgeon on Friday. Long term plan is taking pills and or chemotherapy. As for now I have no limitations, and no special diet. I already eat health; I limit my sweets and fats! Dr. D ordered a CAT scan and a BRCA1, BRCA2. Those are genetic tests to see if I carry a gene for hereditary breast cancer. Its is a concern because I'm 34 and my maternal grandmother died from breast cancer in 1974.

January 18, 2014

Happy Saturday to everyone! I had a consultation with my surgeon yesterday. Surgery will be on Tuesday January 28, 2014. The surgeon recommended for me to have right mastectomy with delayed reconstruction. It's an overnight stay at the VA hospital with a minimum of 2 weeks for recovery. I have a few appointments to go to before the 28th that includes and EKG, bone scan, and some more labs.

January 23, 2014

Good Morning everyone! I am at the VA hospital for a bone scan appointment. I got a radioactive material injection at 9:15am CST and I have to wait 3 hours before I have the pictures taken. This is my first bone scan, so I am explaining briefly the process to anyone who never had it done. It was not a scary experience, and it doesn't' hurt. I also had more blood drawn for the BRCA test (genetic testing done to see if I'm a carrier for the breast cancer gene). Results come in an average of 2-4 weeks, and my oncologist will tell me the results. I am in good spirits today and am trying to remain calm these next few days!!!

January 28, 2014

(Mom) Nikki's surgery went well and a right mastectomy was performed as scheduled. Thank-You all for you continued prayers for Nikki's full recovery. I talked to Nikki a few minutes ago and she sounded good. She will have an overnight stays at the VA hospital and go home tomorrow. Thank-you all for your continued prayers and support!!!!!

January 29, 2014

Good Morning to my FTB (fighting the battle) friends and family! I am being discharged this morning! I just talked to a RN who was able to answer some of my questions. The doctors said I don't need a home health nurse because I don't have bandages, I have ALOT of stitches covered with surgical glue. I have been instructed on how to empty out my JP (Jackson Pratt) drains and measure the liquid. The drains will stay in 1-2 weeks. I had two ladies who work in the X-ray department com visit me an hour ago. One lady had assisted the radiologist technician on January 2 when my biopsy was performed. The other lady did my cat-scan last Thursday. Anyways, they asked me if I wanted crackers or cookies to snack on. I said sure and that the graham crackers were good . The women came back with a plastic bag full of 2 20oz Sprites, Chips Ahoy cookies, and a big bag of Cheetos! It was a nice surprise!!!!!

January 30, 2014
Hi everyone! I'm just waking up from a nap! I got up early with the kids and signed notebooks and looked at schoolwork. I took my meds and ate a light breakfast with juice. VA did call to check up on me. Everyone, (and I know you all are too) is amazed at how well I am doing and moving around! It definitely will take some time to adjust to my new look!! GOD IS GOOD ALL THE TIME, and my appearance does not define who I am. My breast is gone; but I still have my smile and I am full of life!

January 31,2014
Hello everyone! I am happy to announce that I was able to take a bath last night and put on lotion! I feel so much better!! Last Sat-Sun I had to bathe with the pre op soap that left my skin very dry. I had to wait 48 hours post surgery to bathe. I am able to raise my right arm all the way up and rotate it normal; which is really good! I brushed my hair too. These are small tasks but I am healing fairly quick. I know it's the power of prayer and God keeping me in his arms! Thank-you all so much, I am still on restrictions to lifting no more than 10 pounds with my right arm. The JP drains are a pain but they do help get rid of excess fluids. I have to be careful how I move around so I don't rip them out. I will have my surgery check up on Feb 12.

February 19, 2014
(Mom) I talked to Nikki a little while ago and she is doing fine. She's hoping to have more information soon on her chemotherapy and radiation therapy. She is looking forward to going back to work. She'll update her status later. Thank-you all for keeping her in your prayers.

February 20, 2014
I saw my oncologist on Tuesday. The latest news is that I will have to do a radiation consultation at Scott & White in Killeen, because the Temple VA doesn't do that. If radiation is needed I will do that after my chemotherapy is completed. My oncologist is waiting to hear from a doctor with answers on when I will have to take 2 pills after chemotherapy for 5-10 years!!!! This is to make sure the cancer doesn't return. On Monday I have to do an EKG

on my heart to make sure it's healthy enough for me to have a chemo port implanted if I need it. I can't say this enough THANK-YOU ALL FOR YOUR CONTINUED PRAYERS, SUPPORT, AND LOVE!!! Have a great Thursday!

March 14, 2014

Hello and good morning everyone! I know it's been awhile since I posted on here. I have been doing well, I went back to work on March 3. This week I was of for spring break. I'm at the oncologist now, and I hope to get answers on what my options are for chemotherapy. I want to know when it starts, and how long I will have treatments for. My oncologist did call me on Tuesday to tell me my result for the BRCA1 test was negative! That is a big relief to know that I am not a carrier for the breast cancer gene. *Thank-you Lord for all of your blessings and watching over all of your children, Amen.* I will update everyone on what's going on when I am finished my appointment! Have a great day!

March 16, 2014

(Mom) Hi All- Nikki's getting ready for chemo and still showing how BIG her Brave is- she had her hair cut off yesterday to avoid it falling out in clumps. Locks of Love needed her hair to be 10" in order to donate, but its not that long. She will post more soon. Thanks for all you love and prayers for my little girl.

March 19, 2014

(Mom) Nikki had surgery yesterday for the port to be put in her jugular vein to receive her chemo. (Ports are used to deliver chemotherapy to cancer patients who must undergo treatment frequently. Chemotherapy is often toxic, and can damage skin and muscle tissue, and therefore should not be delivered through these tissues. Port-a-caths provide a solution, delivering drugs quickly and efficiently through the entire body via the circulatory system). Nikki sounded good after the procedure and remains positive. Her first chemotherapy treatment is today and either she or I will post later with how she's doing. Thank-you all for keeping those prayers coming her way... And the journey continues.

March 19, 2014

I am at my first chemo appointment. I'm receiving a lot of information about Adriamycin, Cyclophoshamide, and neulasta which is a shot I give myself in the stomach or bottom 24 hours after I receive my chemo treatments. I have some more prescriptions to pick up when I'm done. Anxiety pills, nausea pills, pills to help me sleep at night if for some reason I can't fall asleep. I"m learning a lot today! Prior to any chemo medicine being administered I have my port flushed, then have a nausea IV bag for 15 mins, and them 15 mins of saline. Both treatments take 30 minutes to go through my port.

April 7, 2014

Good Afternoon everyone! I know that it has been a few days since I last posted. My second round of chemotherapy I had on April 2, was more intense than the first round. I am having more side effects now, but that is expected. I am feeling better today than I was feeling on Friday!

April 14, 2014

Happy Monday everyone! I had the rest of my hair cut off on Saturday; the little bit that I had left was falling out! My spirits were lifted on Saturday when I received 3 cards in the mail! One card was from Mary and Jim Manes friends of my mom and Michael from when we lived at the Tobyhanna Army Depot.   The other 2 cards had no return address or signature, but they were stamped from Charleston WV. Thank-you all so much for your card, continued support, love and prayers.

April 15, 2014

Good Morning! More of my spirits were lifted when I checked my mailbox when I came home from work yesterday. I received a postcard from Julia Lewis, Aunt Cindy, Uncle Richard, Linda and John Kerr (thank-you so much for the Walmart gift cards, and your prayer petition!!) Thank-you to Katie, my mom and Wil, my brother Anthony and his girlfriend Ticcorra for their cards. Tomorrow I have my third round of chemo. I'm ready to get this round over with and I pray that I will be feeling better in time for Easter! Have a blessed day!

April 16, 2014

Hump Day! I'm at my third chemo session right now. I'm halfway through my Adriamycin drip. My vitals were normal, and I've lost 7 pounds since I started chemotherapy on 3/19!! I discussed with my oncologist the side effects I have experienced. The bone pain that I have after taking the 6mg Nuelasta shot is excruciating; however it means that it is working!

April 17, 2014

My spirits were lifted high at work this morning at MVES when I was delivered a royal blue box labeled Treasured Keys To Life. I wanted to thank my anonymous gift giver and also for the Walmart gift card! May you and your family have a blessed Easter! Much Love, Nikki Dorman

April 18, 2014

Good morning everyone! May all of you have a Good Friday! I just wanted to let everyone know that my third chemotherapy treatment was successful! My white blood count and hemoglobin levels are both good!!! My oncologist prescribed me 150 mg of Gastro Esophageal reflex pills which works MUCH BETTER than the 4 mg nausea medicine! Dr. D advised me to take my pain pills prior to self-administering my Nuelasta shot to avoid the bone pain I had 2 weeks ago! Dr. D's suggestion worked for me and I'm feeling great today! My body temperature is 97.1 f which is my new normal versus 98.6 f and my BP was 122/72!

April 22, 2014

Thank-you to Michael and Marcia K, and also to my cousins Daliah, Danielle and Janelle for your cards that I received yesterday!!! The cards that I have received help keep me positive and focused on winning my fight!

April 26, 2014

I thought I posted this yesterday; but I didn't so I'm re posting this now. Thank-you to my Mom, Wil, my brother Anthony and his girlfriend Ticorra for my " Box Of Love" I received yesterday! The surprise box contained a cute and cuddly chemo bear, a neat of pair of cushioned headphones that I can use with my iPhone, an inspirational book titled "Real Moments" by Barbara DeAngelis, Ph. D., 2 cozy pink pairs of socks, and some other things to brighten my spirits!!! Thank-you soooooo much!! I hope everyone is having an awesome weekend! I received a beautiful card from my cousin Joyce Harrison... I would like to post what Joyce wrote because it is worth repeating!

Nikki:

> **Every update from you is inspiring! To see that**
> **you can overcome anything handed to you**
> **is an example of how resilient we all should be!**
> **Love You! Joyce   I love you too cousin!!!!**

April 30,2014

Thank-you to Aunt Dawn, Uncle Bill, Billy, Christopher and Thomas for your cards the I received in the mail yesterday!! I had my fourth chemotherapy treatment today, all went well. I do my last shot of Nuelasta Thursday night. I start my next chemotherapy drug May 14, and it's called Taxol, I'm told its not as toxic. If all goes well, them my final chemo will be June 25, 2014!!!!

May 3, 2014
Thank-you to Linda, and John Kerr!!! When I arrived home on Friday there was a package waiting on the porch for me! My spirits were uplifted from the "surprise package"!!!

May 12, 2014
Thank-you to Mr. and Mrs. Katie Saldibar for sending me a "box of love" on Friday. It was a big surprise to see a Scentsy box on the porch! I am new to Scentsy; but I know I will love the pineapple scent, and warmer!! I adore the pink camouflage blanket and cozy tote socks. I can start reading the Chicken Soup for the Soul Cancer Book on Wednesday at my fifth chemotherapy session. Thanks for all the other goodies in the box!!

May 14, 2014
HUMP DAY! HAPPY WEDNESDAY EVERYONE! I'm at my fifth chemotherapy appointment right now. I just started my Taxol drip. There is a Taxol kit on standby, in case I have an allergic reaction to the new medicine. I had a benedryl drip 20 mins ago1 I'm just happy that I'm finished the first of meds and I'm finished with the Nuelasta shot!!! I did have an appointment Tuesday with a mastectomy bra fitter. She was very helpful She was very helpful in getting me the products (mastectomy bra, and a prosthetic boob) I need to help me feel and look normal again!

May 15, 2014
Sporting my new wig!! I got my wig yesterday afternoon at the Fountain of Beauty Salon and Spa in Temple TX. American Cancer Society donates wigs to them and other vendors!

May 19, 2014
Good Morning! I hope everyone had a great weekend! I received a call this morning from the Scott & White Oncology Clinic in Killeen. I have a 6/18 appointment for my radiation consultation. I'm not out of the woods yet, but I'm getting a step closer to being CANCER FREE!!!!!

May 22, 2014
Good Morning everyone! I want to thank Kim Hawkins in Pipestem WV for mailing me out a "box of love"!!! It was waiting on the porch for me! I

love the Cool Gear insulated mug with the option to sip or chug! Some other items in the box were Juicy Fruit gum,Mambo fruit chews, word search book (I love doing these), Subway gift-card, diary book, THIRTY ONE purple bag (my fave color). Thank-you again to EVERYONE for your support, posting your messages on Eye Of The Tiger, and reading my messages, your cards, PRAYERS, AND LOVE!! Thank-you to Mary and Jim for your card I received on Tuesday this week. Here is YOUR THOUGHT FOR TODAY! This is from an unknown author (perhaps you've read it before)

LIVE EACH DAY WITH GRATITUDE

Gratitude is one of life's greatest gifts and is free for the choosing. When we make this choice, we are demonstrating an understanding in our free will.

Gratitude is a practice...an exercise in which we train our minds to look at the good things before us each day, no matter what is happening in our lives.

Gratitude is a state of mind we cultivate in ourselves that enables us to understand that often it is our greatest challenges and loses that brings us our greatest lessons.

Gratitude is the place from which we recognize life's compensations that are always before us, so we can enjoy each day with thanksgiving.

May 28, 2014
Hi everyone1 I just completed my sixth chemotherapy treatment today! 2 more to go1 I was prescribed nerve pain medicine, so when I get the fibromyalgia like pain it should help. My doctor put in a consultation with the plastic surgeon. I should be receiving a call for that appointment soon, and I will go from there! All my vitals and labs looked great! Praise The Lord! Thank-you shout out to Michelle Meaney-Demarsh who contacted Jersey Shore Huggers. This company sent me two crocheted hats. One is pink and the other is navy blue!

June 4, 2014
I didn't have have any chemotherapy today, but I am down to my last 2 treatments!!! June 11 and June 25!! My radiation consultation is on June 18, and I have a plastic surgeon consultation on June 20. I'm praying that I don't need radiation but if I do, I hope that it won't be lengthy treatment. Good Morning everyone! I hope everyone's Wednesday is going GREAT!! On

Tuesday I received a "box of love", from my cousin Daliah Jones Holmes, and her daughters' Danielle, and Janelle! The box contained a beautiful wicker storage box that contained a subway gift card, Jolly Ranchers, peppermints, 2 fold able water bottles (pretty neat!), an inspirational card, and a blistek.

June 6, 2014

Hello everyone, I hope you all had a great Friday! I received a "box of love" from Michelle-Demarsh on Thursday!! The box contained an orange Calvin Klein Scarf, pajamas in a bottle, and a bottle of massaging lotion. The lotion was relaxation lotion that has lavender and chamomile.

June 8, 2014

Another fantastic, thoughtful, spirit lifting, "box of love" arrived on Saturday from Linda and John Kerr!!! In the box I found a cute pink Beanie Baby named Promise, who is wearing the ribbon of hope! A CD called HOPE-songs to celebrate life, a Hallmark Keepsake ornament- Snowman Angel wearing a pink knitted scarf on the bottom of the snowman it says: Surrounded By Caring, notepad and pen, N stationary that is pink, a musical card that is very nice! Saving the best for last.... I received another ornament that is a Waterford Crystal, absolutely beautiful! Thank-you so much Linda and John!!!

June 10, 2014

It's the end of the school year- Let the summer begin!

June 11, 2014

GM everyone! I want to thank Amanda and Antoine Robinson for their card, and Target gift card! Thank-you Mike Kulikowski Jr. for your note!

June 16 2014

Hi everyone! I received a surprise "box of love" from Julia Lewis on Saturday! The box included; A Nivea Kiss Collection 3 lip butters, and 2 lip care sticks with SPF. Raspberry, Cranberry, and Blueberry Tea. Two books... 1) Be Unique-Peanuts Wisdom to Carry You Through 2) Life Songs-Giving Voice To The Spirit Within, and a nice purple fashion scarf!

Thank-you again Julia Lewis! Wishing everyone a blessed week! I will be updating everyone after my appointments on Wednesday and Friday this week!

June 18, 2014

Good evening everyone! Today I had my radiation consultation, the doctor told me because of the results of my pathology and age that I MUST undergo radiation. It's not the end of the world, but that's not what I wanted to hear. I will start radiation at the end of July, for 30 treatments. I will be going Monday-Friday for 6 weeks. This radiation therapy will postpone my reconstruction surgery for 6 months after the last treatment.

June 21, 2014

Hi everyone! Just an update about my appointment with the plastic surgeon. Without me going into too much detail, I can choose between 2 different surgeries. One being a simpler procedure that the other, and with less healing time. I will be praying on everything. I have a follow up appointment in December with the doctor and to make my final decision! Right now I'm just excited and prepared for my final chemotherapy on Wednesday June 25, 2014! One step at a time, another chapter completed in my book of life! Have a great weekend!!!

June 25, 2014

Hi everyone! Happy Hump Day! I'm at my final chemotherapy appointment! I'm blessed to have conquered 8 rounds of chemotherapy every 2 weeks! Another blessing was being able to go to work the next day after each chemotherapy treatment to cross the children at MVES! Many people are in bed a few days after chemotherapy!

This is another major milestone in my life! I couldn't have gone through this journey alone! The power of prayer (everyone's prayers of all religions), boxes of love, cards and gifts! Today is a celebration of new life, new dreams, and so much more! My Aunt Dee came with me today for my last chemotherapy, and my daughter Anastazija made me my final chemotherapy poster!

June 26, 2014

A big Thank-You to Ameisha Jo Boone for mailing me a "box of love"1 I received her package on Saturday. The package contained mascara, 2 nail polishes, candy, picture frames, a Beautiful Willow Tree Loving Angel, and a Bath and Body Works lotion, spray, and bath gel! Thank-You again Ameisha!

July 3, 2014

Wishing everyone a happy and safe 4th of July! I am looking forward to seeing how much my new hair grows in weekly! It is very light, and fuzzy!

July 10, 2014

I'm over joyous to report that I had a CAT Scan done today at the Temple VA. My oncologist called me at 11:46am to let me know that everything looked good, and that there are **NO CANCER CELLS** in my body!!!!! It has been said so many times before, and it is worth repeating! **God Is Good All The Time, All Time God Is Good!** When I had my final chemotherapy on June 25, I requested to have the CAT scan done so I could have peace of mind. I still have to go through the radiation treatments for 6 weeks starting the end of July. My new hair continues to grow in, I will be posting weekly pictures on my Eye Of The Tiger Facebook page for everyone to see my hair growth progress. I received a "box of love" from Cheryl Davis July 9th, her package contained a word search book and pencil, 3 fruit flavored soaps, and a Thomas Kinkade Gospel Songs CD! Thank-You so much Cheryl Davis for thinking about me! I encourage all of my female friends and family no matter what you age is... if you detect a lump, don't delay please get it checked out! 40 is NOT the age to start getting mammograms, that is not the case anymore. Sadly enough, females are being diagnosed with breast cancer as young as in their teen! Also breast cancer is not as common in men but you men can have breast cancer too! So remember, when in doubt, get that lump checked out!

July 16, 2014

Good afternoon everyone! Today I had my radiation CT simulation. I will begin radiation daily on July 30 for 6 weeks. My radiologist doctor gave me an information packet with possible short and long term side effects.

July 22, 2014

I would like to send a BIG thank-you to Linda and John Kerr for sending another FANTASTIC "BOX OF LOVE" for children Anastazija, Marcos, and Caesar. I was completely blown away when I opened the box and seen three personalized bags for school, and school supplies. My children will go back to school with these unique initialed Thirty-One bags!

July 31, 2014

Hello everyone! My first radiation appointment went well yesterday. I had to lay on a table. The area being treated was drawn on with a sharpie. I have a few clear stickers on me that I have to leave on for the duration of the treatment period of 6 weeks. I had to get x-rays done of the areas I'm having radiation on. The areas being treated are on the right side of my neck, collar bone, and mastectomy site. I have to lay on the table with my arms above my head holding onto a bar. A gel material is placed on my chest and then the radiologist tech leaves the room. A machine with a red beam goes over the site being treated for 10 minutes. I was there for 45 minutes yesterday because of the set up, and x-rays. My radiologist oncologist told me of that some side effects I may get are fatigue, darkening of the skin, and peeling of skin over time. Other side effects that people experience are blisters, but I pray that I will not get them! I also have to use mild soap and lotions on the treatment sites.

August 15, 2014

Hi everyone! I'm doing great, and feeling wonderful! Radiation is going well, I've had 13 treatments so far, and 17 more to go! I feel a little fatigued, but its not as bad ad chemotherapy was. Radiation is a walk in the park in comparison!

September 11, 2014

Hello everyone! I know its been a while since I've written on here, and I apologize. Yesterday I completed my radiation treatments. On the flip side I do have many painful radiation burns, and swelling. My skin started to peel last Friday, but my doctor says I should be completely healed in 2-4 weeks. I have been educated about proper skin care and I am taking pain medicine at night. Another chapter of my breast cancer journey is completed!

September 25, 2014

Hi everyone! I hope everyone is doing well and that your all in good health and spirits! I had an appointment at the Temple VA on Monday with my oncologist. I had last seen her on June 25 for my last chemotherapy. Dr. D said that I looked good, and that my labs were good. I was prescribed Tamoxifen. Tamoxifen is the 20 mg pill that I will take daily for 5+ years! It's whatever it takes to stay healthy right? After all taking a pill is nothing compared to conquering surgeries, chemotherapy, and radiation! I had a follow-up with my radiologist yesterday for my 2 week follow up. She said my new skin growth looks good. I'm still peeling a little bit, but I am not in pain like I was. For those of you who don't know, having your skin peel from having radiation treatments, is not the same as getting a sunburn and peeling!

October 6, 2014
To all women and men who are battling any type of cancer, keep fighting the fight! Don't give up! Your not in your journey alone! The cancer fight is quite a challenge, but with help, support, and love from friends/ family, and your medical team you can win the fight! I can testify to that! Thank-you to everyone who has supported me throughout my continuous journey!

Anastanzja Bingham
11/26/2014

Eye of the Tiger

Jan 7 2014   A week before Nikki's 35th birthday test results of her biopsy show she has a form of breast cancer. We are using this group page for support and to keep family and friends updated on her progress. Nikki is in good spirits and will get more information from her doctors next week. ... And the journey begins. Thank you Jesus for being with us all throughout this journey.

Jan 10 2014   Good Morning Everyone! Words cannot express how blessed, and thankful I am to have such a great support group. I will send updates when I have Appts, etc. I am in good spirits and feeling GREAT today!!

Jan 11 2014   Hi Family and Friends,

The latest update is: since I did not hear from the oncologist I called the department and asked when my first appointment is.... Jan 14, @ 2pm. I was told it is a Q&A appointment and information on what's going to happen from here on out!

I have just created my own campaign page titled Support Nikki's Fight.... I have more details about the type of breast cancer I have. In addition I'm trying to raise money to help pay bills. I read that any type of cancer is an expensive illness. Please encourage your FB friends and family to check it out. You can find my campaign page on FundRazr.com, and do a search for Nicole Dorman my pic is there. Donations can be made by PayPal. I plan to donate some of my proceeds to Saint Jude's Children's Hospital. Have a good weekend everyone and I Love You all for your prayers!

Jan 11 2014 Help Support Nikki's Fight With Breast Cancer!

Hi Everyone,

I am Nicole Dorman, 34, and will be 35 January 15, 2014. I had a core needle breast biopsy on Jan 2, 2014. I received a phone call January 7, 2014 in the afternoon, the results were positive and I was diagnosed with Invasive Ductal Carcinoma. It's a form of breast cancer that can spread throughout my body. It normally affects men and women who are over 45! **On January 2, 2014 I had a right mastectomy,** I am off work until March 3, 2014 to heal and have follow up appointments with my surgeon, and oncologist. I am a single mom to 3 kids ages 6, 8, and 14. I am their sole provider and I cannot let this cancer defeat me! On February 7, 2014 my pathology report stated that I am at Stage 2b. I work part-time for a Texas School as a crossing guard, my job is physical but I love it! My monthly income is $1,100 barely enough to pay rent, utilities, phone bill, and other expenses that arise. I don't have a car, but I get to work to be able to provide for my kids. I am going to be treated at a Texas VA Hospital because I am a Army Veteran. My medical is being taken care but I do have to pay for any prescriptions. I am asking everyone that can to please donate any amout you can to help me and my young children.   Your contributions will be greatly appreciate and used towards my monthly bills, getting to my appointments, and prescriptions! I plan to donate a portion of my donations to St. Jude's Children's Research Hospital! Thank-you and God Bless!

Jan 13 2014   Happy Monday Everyone! Hope you all had a great weekend! My weekend was great. Anastazija, Marcos, and Caesar stayed at a friend's house Saturday. I went and did some grocery shopping at HEB, went to Walmart, and had dinner at Applebee's! Sunday was more of a relaxed day where I ironed my clothes, and the boys' clothes for this week. I was going to wait until Tuesday night but I didn't want to overload them with information. Annie took the news the hardest, and Caesar is too young to understand what's going on. I assured them that my illness is not there fault, and that I love them very much!

Jan 13 2014   The ball is moving....... I had my blood draws and had to give a U sample at 7am. Now I am at my primary physician waiting to see Dr. Lopez, who is a female so it makes it easier to talk to another women. I received a phone from VA appointments to tell me I have a surgery consult on Friday at 11am. I will write more after my appt at 9:30am.

Jan 14 2014   Hi Everyone! Here is the latest update: I met with my oncologist Dr.Dodlapati (female). She allowed me to look over my biopsy and ultrasound results while she translated what everything meant. At this time she doesn't know what stage I'm at because a lymph **node has to be taken out during surgery and tested. The mass is 2.5cmx2cm (over 1inch long** and wide) I am at grade 1 which is good, meaning it doesn't look like the cancer cells have spread beyond my right breast. I do have a lot calcification (cancer cells that are old but not invasive). Dr. D says that my short term plan is surgery lumpectomy followed by radiation, or mastectomy. I will find out more about that when I meet with the surgeon Friday. Long term plan is pills or chemo. As for now I have no limitations, and no special diet. I already eat healthy regularly and limit my sweets and fats! Dr. D ordered a CAT scan and a BRCA1, and BRCA2. Those are generic tests to see if I carry a gene for hereditary breast cancer. It is a concern because I'm 34 and my grandma (RIP) died at 48 from breast cancer.

January 15 Nikki's 35th Birthday

Jan 18 2014   Happy Saturday to everyone! I had my consultation with my surgeon yesterday. Surgery will be on Tuesday January 28. The surgeon recommended for me to have a mastectomy with delayed reconstruction. It's an overnight stay at the VA hospital with a minimum of 2 weeks for recovery. I have a few appointments to go to before the 28th that includes an EKG, bone scan , and some more labs.

Jan 23 2014   Good Morning Everyone! I am at the VA for a bone scan appointment. I got the radioactive material injection at 9:15am central time and I have to wait 3 hours before I have the pictures taken. This is my first bone scan, so I was explaining briefly the process to anyone who never had it done. I also had more blood drawn for the BRCA test (genetic testing done see if I'm a carrier for breast cancer gene). Results come in 2-4 weeks, and my oncologist will tell me the results. I am in good spirits today and am trying to remain calm these next few days!!!

Have a blessed day!

Jan 28 2014 *Photo Posted* (pam) Nikki's surgery went well and right mastectomy was performed as scheduled. Thank you all for your continued prayers for Nikki's full recovery. I talked to Nikki a few minutes ago and she sounded good She will have an overnight stay at the VA Hospital and go home tomorrow. Thank you for your continued prayers for my little girl.

Jan 28 2014 Prayer is very powerful!!! I have God to thank for having a successful surgery and I pray for a speedy recovery. God bless all of my family and friends, and co-workers for all of their prayers and support!!!!!!!

Jan 29 2014 Good Morning To My FTB (fighting the battle) friends and family! I am being discharged this morning! I just talked to a RN who was able to answer some of my questions. The doctors said I don't need a home health nurse because I don't have bandages, I have ALOT of stitches covered with surgical glue. I have been instructed on how to empty out my JP drains and measure the liquid. The drains will stay in 1-2 weeks. I had two ladies who work in the X-ray department come visit me an hour ago. One lady assisted the radiologist technician on Jan 2, 2014 when my biopsy was done, and the other lady did my cat scan last Thursday. Anyways, they asked me if I wanted crackers or cookies to snack on, I said sure and that the graham crackers were good. They came back with a plastic bag full of 2 20 oz sprites, chips ahoy cookies, big bag of Cheetos and some crackers from the cafeteria! It was a nice surprise!

Jan 30 2014 Hi Everyone! I'm just waking up from a nap! I got up early with the kids and signed notebooks and looked at schoolwork. I took my meds and ate a light breakfast with juice. VA did call to check up on me. Everyone, (and I know you all are too) is amazed at how well I am doing and moving around! It definitely will take some time to adjust to my new look!!! GOD IS GOOD ALL THE TIME, and my appearance does not define who I am. My breast is gone but I still have my smile, and am full of life!

Jan 31 2014 Hello everyone! I am happy to announce that I was able to take a bath last night and put on lotion!!!! I feel so much better! Last Sat- Sun I had to bath with pre op soap that left my skin VERY dry. I had to wait 48 hours post surgery to bathe. I am able to raise my right arm all the way up and rotate it as normal which is really good! I brushed my hair too. These are small tasks but I am healing fairly quickly! I know it's the power of prayer, and God **keeping me in his arms! Thank-you all so much. I am still on restrictions to lifting no more** than 10 pounds with my right arm. The JP drains are a pain but they help get rid of excess fluids. I have to be careful how I move around so I don't rip them out. I will have my post surgery check up Feb, 12.

Feb 19 2014 (pam) I talked to Nikki a little while ago and she's doing fine. She's hoping to have more information soon on her treatment plan re chemo and radiation therapy and she's looking forward to going back to work. She'll update her status later. Thank you all for keeping her in your prayers

Feb 20 2014   Good Morning Everyone,

I saw my oncologist on Tuesday. Latest news is I will have to do a radiation consultation at Scott and White in Killeen because the Temple VA doesn't do that. If radiation is needed I will do that after my chemotherapy is completed. My oncologist is waiting to hear from a doctor with answers on when I would start chemo and for how long (something on my pathology report is questionable) I will have to take 2 pills after chemo for 5-10 years!!!! This is to make sure the cancer doesn't return. On Monday I have to do an EKG on my heart to make sure it's healthy enough for me to have a chemo port implanted if I need it!   I can't say this enough THANK-YOU ALL FOR YOUR CONTINUED PRAYERS, SUPPORT, AND LOVE!!!!! Have a great Thursday!

March 14 2014 Hello and good morning everyone! I know it's been a while since I posted on here. I have been doing good, I went back to work March 3. This week I was off for spring break. I'm at the oncologist now. I hope to get answers on what my options are for chemo, and when that starts, how long etc. My oncologist did call me on Tuesday to tell me my result for the BRCA1 test was negative! That is a big relief to know that I am not carrier for the **breast cancer gene! Thank-you Lord for all your blessings and watching over all your children!** Amen!!!!! I will update everyone on what's going on when I am finished my appointments! Have a great day!

March 16 2014   (photo posted of micro haircut ~ preparing for chemo)

I'm feeling great now but will post on here later to let you all know how I'm feeling.

March 16 2014   (pam)   Hi All ~ Nikki's getting ready for chemo and still showing how BIG her Brave is ~ she had her hair cut off yesterday to avoid it falling out in clumps. Locks of Love needed her hair to be 10" in order to donate but it's not that long. She will post more soon. Thanks for all your love and prayers for my little girl. Nikki had a bit of trouble with her phone so I'm posting these gorgeous pictures for her

 March 19 2014   (pam) Nikki had surgery yesterday for the port to be put in her jugular vein to receive her chemo. (Ports are used to deliver chemotherapy to cancer patients who must undergo treatment frequently. Chemotherapy is often toxic, and can damage skin and muscle tissue, and therefore should not be delivered through these tissues. Portacaths provide a solution, delivering drugs quickly and efficiently through the entire body via the circulatory system). She sounded good after the procedure and remains positive. Her first chemotherapy treatment is today and either she or I will post later with how she's doing. Thank you all for keeping those prayers coming her way ... And the journey continues.

March 19 2014   I am at my first chemo appt! I'm receiving A LOT of information about Adriamycin, cyclophosphamide, and neulasta which is a shot I give myself in my stomach or bottom 24 hours after I receive my chemo treatments. I have some more prescriptions to pick up when I'm done. Anxiety pills, nausea pills, pills to help me sleep at night if for some reason I can't fall asleep. I'm learning a lot today! Prior to any chemo medicine being administered I have my port flushed, then have a Nausea IV bag (15 min). 15 mins of saline. Both treatments take 30 mins each to go through my port.

(photo posted) 1st chemo session! You can see where my port is. My chest and neck are still very sore!

April 2 2014 Hi Everyone! I'm at the Temple TX VA Hospital getting my second round of chemo! My oncologist put me on stronger nausea medicine to take. i did loose my appetite a few times. I have not had any other side effects! (Knock on wood) I did loose 1 lb lol so far in 2 weeks. Dr. D recommend me to do more stretching and walking but no strenuous exercises.

April 7 2014 Good Afternoon Everyone! I know it's been a few days since I last posted. My second round of chemo on April 2, was more harder than the first round on March 19th. I am having more side effects than the last time ,but that is expected. I am feeling better today than Friday!

April 14 2014 (photo posted) Happy Monday everyone! I had the rest of my hair cut off is Saturday. The little bit that I had left was falling out!

My spirits were lifted on Saturday when I received 3 cards in the mail!!!! One was from Mary and Jim Maness friends of my mom and Michael from when we lived at the Tobyhanna Army Depot. The other 2 cards had no return address or signature, but they were stamped from Charleston WV. Thank-you all so much for your cards, continued support, love, and prayers.

April 15 2014 Good Morning! More of my spirits were lifted when I checked my mailbox when I came home from work yesterday. I received a postcard from Julia Lewis, Aunt Cindy, Uncle Richard, Linda and John Kerr (thank-you so much for the WalMart Gift Cards, and your prayer petition!!) Thank-you to Katie, my Mom, Wil, my brother Anthony, and his girlfriend Ticcorra for their cards. Tomorrow I have my 3rd round of chemo. I'm ready to get this round over with, and I pray that I will be feeling better in time for Easter! Have a blessed Day!!!!

April 16 2014 Hump Day! I'm at my 3 rd chemo session right now halfway thru my adriamycin drip! My vitals were all normal. I have lost 7 pounds since I started chemo on 3/19!!!!! I discussed with my oncologist the side effects I been having. The bone pain that I have after taking the 6 mg Nuelasta shot is excruciating!!!!!! However, it means that it Is working.

April 18 2014 My spirits were lifted high this morning when I was delivered royal blue box labeled Treasured Keys To Life. I wanted to thank my anonymous gift giver, and also for the Walmart Gift Card!! May you and your family have a blessed Easter! Much Love, Nikki Dorman

I asked the assistant principal of my school I work at and volunteer at to send an email out to all of the employees with the same message I just posted!

April 18 2014 Good Morning Everyone! May all of you have a Good Friday! Just wanted to let everyone know that my 3rd chemo treatment was successful! My white blood count and hemoglobin levels are both good!!!!! My oncologist put me on 150 mg of Gastro Esophageal reflux pills which works MUCH BETTER than the 4mg nausea medicine! She advised me to take my pain pills prior to self administering my Nuelasta shot to avoid the bone pain I had 2 weeks ago! That worked and am feeling great today! My body temp is 97.1 which is my new normal versus the 98.6 and my bp was 122/72 !

April 22 2014   Thank-you to Michael and Marcia and my cousins Daliah, Danielle and Janelle for your cards that I received yesterday!!!! The cards that I have received help to keep me positive, and focused on my fight!

April 26 2014   I thought this posted yesterday.... But it didn't so I am reposting now. Thank-You to my Mom, Wil, Anthony and Ticorra for my "Box of Love" I received yesterday! The surprise box contained a cute and cuddly chemo bear, a neat pair of cushioned headphones that I can use with my iPhone (I don't like ear buds I don't use the pair that came with my phone), an inspirational book titled "Real Moments" by Barbara DeAngelis, Ph.D.,2 cozy pink pairs of socks, and some other things to brighten my spirits!!!! Thank-you soooooo much!

I hope everyone is having a awesome weekend! I received a beautiful card from my cousin Joyce Harrison..... I would like to post what Joyce wrote because it is worth repeating!

Nikki:

Every update from you is inspiring! To see that you can overcome anything handed to you is an example of how resultant we all should be!

Love you!   Joyce

Love you too cousin!!!!

April 30 2014 Thank-you to Aunt Dawn, Uncle Bill, Billy, Christopher and Thomas for your cards that I received in the mail yesterday!!!!!!!!!!!

I had my 4th treatment today, all went well. I do my last shot of Nuelasta Thursday night. I start my next chemo drug May 14, and its called Taxol, I'm told its not as toxic. If all goes well then my final chemo will be June 25!!!!!!!!!

May 3 2014 Thank-you to Linda and John Kerr! When I arrived home on Friday there was a package waiting on the porch for me! My spirits were uplifted from the "surprise package"!!!!!

May 12 2014   Thank-you to Mr. And Katie Mrs. Saldibar for sending me a Box Of Love on Friday. It was a big surprise to see a Scentsy box on the porch! I am new to Scentsy but I know I will love the pineapple scent, and warmer! !!!!!! I adore the pink camouflage blanket and cozy tote socks. I can start reading the Chicken Soup For the Soul Cancer Book on Wed at my 5th chemo session. Thanks for the other goodies in the box!!!!!

May 14 2014   HUMP DAY! HAPPY WEDNESDAY EVERYONE! I'm at my 5th chemotherapy appointment right now. I just started my Taxol drip. There is a Taxol kit on standby, incase I have an allergic reaction to the new med. I had a Benedryl drip 20 mins ago! I'm just happy that I am finished the first to meds and I'm done with the Nuelasta shot!!!!!

I did have an appointment Tuesday with a mastectomy fitter. She was very helpful in getting me the products I need to help me feel normal again!

May 15 2014 **photo posted** Sporting my new wig!!!!! I got it yesterday at the Fountain Of Beauty Salon and Spa in Temple TX. American Cancer Society donates wigs to them and other vendors!

May 19 2014 Good Morning! Hope everyone had a great weekend!! I received a call this morning from the Scott & White Oncology Clinic in Killeen. I have a 6/18 appointment for my radiation consultation. I'm not out of the woods yet, but I'm getting a step closer to being CANCER FREE!

May 22 2014 Good Morning Everyone! I want to thank Kim Hawkins in Pipestem WV for mailing me out a box of love!!!!! It was waiting on the porch for me! I love the COOL GEAR insulated mug with option to sip or chug! Lol. Some other items in the box were Juicy Fruit gum, Mambo fruit chews, word search book (love doing these!), Subway gift-card, diary book, THIRTY ONE purple bag (my fave color) Thank -You again to EVERYONE for you support, posting messages on Eye Of The Tiger, viewing messages on Eye Of The Tiger, your cards, PRAYER, LOVE!!!!! THANK- YOU to Mary and Jim for your card I received on Tuesday this week.

Here is YOUR THOUGHT FOR TODAY! This is from an unknown author (maybe you've read it before)

LIVE EACH DAY WITH GRATITUDE

Gratitude is one of life's greatest gifts and is free for the choosing. When we make this choice, we are demonstrating an understanding I'd our free will.

Gratitude is a practice...an exercise in which we train our minds to look at the good things before us each day, no matter what is happening in our lives.

Gratitude is a state of mind we cultivate in ourselves that enables us to understand that often it is our greatest challenges and losses that brings us our greatest lessons.

Gratitude is the place from which we recognize life's compensations that are always before us, so we can enjoy each day with thanksgiving.

May 28 2014 Hi everyone! I just completed my 6th chemo treatment today! 2 more to go! I was prescribed nerve pain med, so when I get the fibromyalgia like pain it should help. My doctor put in a consultation with the plastic surgeon so I should be receiving a call for that appointment soon and go from there! All my vitals and labs looked good, Praise The Lord!

Eye of the Tiger ~

Thank-You shout out to Michelle Meaney-Demarsh who contacted Jersey Shore Huggers. This company sent me two crocheted hats . One is pink and one is navy blue!

June 4 2014   I didn't have any chemo today, but I am down to my last 2 treatments!!!!! June 11th and 25th!!! My radiation consultation is on June 18th, and I have a plastic surgeon consultation on June 20th! I am praying that I don't need radiation but if I do , hopefully it won't be a lengthy treatment!!!!

Good Morning everyone! I hope everyone's Wednesday is going GREAT. I just wanted to post to let everyone know that I am feeling great !

On Tuesday I received a box of love from my cousin Daliah Jones Holmes and her daughters' Danielle and Janelle! The box contained a beautiful wicker storage box that contained a subway gift card, jolly ranchers, peppermints, 2 foldable water bottles (pretty neat!) a inspirational card, and a blistek.

June 6 2014   Hello Everyone, I hope you all had a great Friday! I received a box of love from Michelle-Demarsh on Thursday!!!! The box contained an orange Calvin Klein scarf, a bottle if massaging lotion, and pajamas In a bottle! It's relaxation lotion that has lavender and chamomile ! Other surprise goodies included a bar of acai berry soap..........and........drum roll please....

Sorry for the delay, my phone is acting up...

I love this awesome personalized Thirty-One bag Michelle!!!!!! Thank-You so much!!!!!

June 8 2014   Another Fantastic, thoughtful, spirit lifting, box of love arrived on Saturday from Linda and John Kerr!!!!!! In the box I found a cute pink Beanie Baby named Promise. She is wearing the pink ribbon!!!! A cd called HOPE- songs to celebrate life, Hallmark Keepsake Ornament - Snowman Angel wearing a pink knitted scarf on the bottom of the snowman it says: Surrounded By Caring. Notepad and pen, N stationary that is pink, a musical card that is very nice! Saving the best for last........ I received another ornament that is a Waterford Crystal, absolutely beautiful! Thank-you sooooooooo much Linda and John!!!!!

June 10 2014 (photo posted) It's the end of the school year ~ Let the summer begin

June 11 2014   GM everyone! I want to thank Amanda and Antwoine Robinson for their card, and Target GC! Also thank you to Mike Kulikowski Jr. for your note!

June 16 2014   Hi Everyone,

I received a surprise box of love from Julia Lewis on Saturday! The box included: A Nivea Kiss

Collection 3 lip butters, and 2 lip care sticks with SPF. Raspberry, Cranberry, and, Blueberry Tea, and a honey bear. Two books.....1) Be Unique- Peanuts Wisdom to Carry You Through 2) Life Songs- Giving Voice To The Spirit Within, and a nice purple fashion scarf! Thank-you again Julia!

Wishing everyone a Blessed Week! I will be updating everyone after my appts on Wednesday, and Friday this week!!

June 18 2014   Good Evening Everyone! Today I had my radiation consultation. The doctor told me because of the results of my pathology report and my age, I must undergo radiation. It's not the end of the world, but that's not what I wanted to hear! I will start radiation the end of July, for 30 treatments. So I will be going Mon-Fri for 6 weeks. This radiation therapy will postpone my reconstruction surgery for 6 months after the last treatment.

June 21 2014   Hi Everyone! Just an update about my appointment with the plastic surgeon. Without going into too much details, I can choose between 2 different surgeries. 1 being a simpler procedure than the other

And less healing time. I will be praying on everything. I have a follow up appt in Dec with the doctor and to make my final decision!!! Right now I'm just excited and prepared for my final chemo on Wed June 25th!!!!!! One step at a time, another chapter completed in my book of life!

Have a great weekend!

June 25 201   *Several photos posted* Hi Everyone! Happy Hump Day!!

I'm at my final chemo appointment! I am blessed to have conquered 8 rounds of chemo every 2 weeks! This is another milestone in my life! I couldn't have done it alone. Today is a celebration of new life, dreams, and the power of prayer!!!! Can I get a Amen?!

I will post the pics. My Aunt Dee-Dee brought me here today! BTW my daughter Anastazija made me a poster!

June 26 2014   A big Thank-You to Ameisha Jo Boone for mailing me a Box Of Love! I received your package on Saturday. The package contained Mascara, 2 nail polishes, candy, pic frames, a BEAUTIFUL Willow Tree Loving Angel, and Bath and Body Works lotion, spray, and bath gel! Thank You again Amisha!

July 3 2014 (photos posted)   Wishing Everyone a Happy and SAFE 4th of July! Here are two pics of my blonde hair coming in, it's very light!!!!! . I'm looking forward to seeing how much it grows in weekly!

July 10 2014   Happy Thursday Everyone!

I am over joyous, to report that I had a CAT Scan done today at the VA. My oncologist called me at 11:46am to let me know that everything looked good, and that there are NO CANCER

CELLS in my body! It has been said so many times before, and is worth repeating! God Is Good, All The Time!

When i had my final chemo on June 25th I requested to have the CAT SCAN done so I could have piece of mind. I still have to go through radiation treatments for 6 weeks starting the end of July. My new hair continues to grow in, I will be posting weekly pictures, for everyone to see my hair growth progress!

I received a box of love from Cheryl Davis July 9th! Her package contained, a word search book and pencil, 3 fruit flavored soaps, Thomas Kinkade Gospel Songs CD! Thank-You so much Cheryl!

Before I post this for today.......

I encourage all my female friends and family no matter what your age is.....If you detect a lump,don't delay please get it checked out! 40 is not the age to start getting mammograms, that is not the case anymore. Sadly enough females are being diagnosed with BC as young as in their teens! Also BC is not as common in men, but men can get it too, so remember "When in doubt, get that lump checked out!"

July 16 2014 (photo posted) Good Afternoon everyone, Today I had my radiation CT simulation. I will begin radiation daily on July 30th for 6 weeks. My radiologist Dr. have me an information packet with possible short and long time side effects. Here is my hair pic for this week!

July 22 2014 I would like to send a HUGE thank-you to Linda and John Kerr for sending another FANTASTIC BOX OF LOVE for my Children. I was completely blown away when I opened the box and seen three personalized bags for school, and school supplies. Anastazija, Marcos, and Caesar will go back to school with these unique initialed Thirty-One bags!!!!!!

P.S. I will definitely be wearing the breast cancer ribbon lanyard, and Thirty-One I.D. Card holder when I return back to work August 25th!!!!

July 24 2014 (photo posted) Here is my artistic daughter Anastazija, showing her special Spider-Man drawing for Danny Nickerson. He is the little boy who turns 6 tomorrow. Danny has an inoperative brain tumor, and wanted nothing but cards for his 6th birthday. We are mailing out his birthday drawing today!

July 31 2014 Hello Everyone! Throwback Thursday!!!!!!

My first radiation appointment went well yesterday. I had to lay on a table. The area being treated was drawn on with a sharpie. I have a few clear stickers on me that I have to leave on for the duration of the treatment period of 6 weeks. I had to get x-rays done of the areas I'm having radiation on. The areas being treated are on the right side of my neck, collar bone, and mastectomy site. I have to lay on the table with my arms above my head holding onto a bar. A gel material is placed on my chest and then the radiologist technologist leave the room. A machine with a red beam goes over the site being treated for 10 mins. I was there for 45 mins yesterday because of the set up, and x-rays. My radiologist oncologist told me that some side effects I may get are fatigue, darkening of the skin, and peeling of the skin (over time). Of course there are other side effects that other people have experienced like blisters, but I pray that I will not have that!!!!! I have to use a mild soap and lotions on the treatment sites, I will have radiation daily for 6 weeks.

Have a great day everyone!

July 30 2014 (photo posted)   This is my selfie for today July 30, 2014.

August 15 2014 (photo posted) Hi Everyone!!!!! I am doing great, and feeling good! Radiation is going good, I have had 13 treatments so far, 17 more to go! I feel a little fatigue but its not as bad as chemo was. Radiation is a walk in the park in comparison! "Hair" are my shots for this week! LOL

September 11 2014   Hello everyone! I know it's been awhile since I've written on here, I apologize. Yesterday I finished my radiation treatments! I have had 30 treatments total. On the flip side I do have a lot of painful radiation burns, and swelling. My skin started peeling last Friday. My doctor said I should be healed in 2-4 weeks. I have been briefed on skin care, and am taking pain medicine at night!

Another chapter of my breast cancer journey is completed! God is good!!!!!

September 25 2014   Hi everyone! I hope everyone is doing good and that your all in good health! It's been a min since I posted a selfie. Last one I posted of my hair growth process was around 5 weeks ago. So here is a pic of me I took today! I had an appt at the VA on Monday with my oncologist. I last seen her on 6-25-14 for my last chemo. She said that I looked good, labs were good, and she prescribed my prescription for Tamoxifen. That's the pill I have to take daily for 5 years!!!!! It's whatever it takes to stay healthy right! After all taking a pill is nothing compared to conquering surgery, chemo, and radiation!!!!!!!

I had a follow up with my radiologist yesterday for my 2 week follow up. She said my new skin growth looks good. I'm still peeling a little bit, but i am not in pain like I was.

October 6 2014 (photo posted) TO ALL WOMEN WHO ARE BATTLING BREAST CANCER, KEEP FIGHTING THE FIGHT! THE CANCER FIGHT IS A CHALLENGE, BUT WITH HELP, SUPPORT, AND LOVE FROM FRIENDS AND FAMILY THE FIGHT CAN BE WON! I CAN TESTIFY TO THAT! THANK-YOU TO EVERYONE WHO HAS SUPPORTED ME THROUGH MY JOURNEY

" Nikki Won The Fight "

October 12 2014 (photo posted) Selfie with pink ribbbon on cheek

October 27 2014 (newspaper photo posted)   I wanted to share this newspaper article with everyone. I took a pic of it so I hope that you can read most of the article!

Dearest Nicole,

Your presence lights up the whole school. I enjoy seeing you work so hard in your job. You have such a sweetness about you. You are very kind and patient.

You put a smile on my face. I am so inspired by your courage and optimism. I wish the very best for you and your family. Your boys are beautiful. Thank you for blessing us all.

Love, Emily Dalling & Family

Love and Hugs

To: Annie
Marcos
&

Cousan

1-28-14

Nikki —

People who know
where your journey started
are happy to see
how far you've come,
how strong and determined
you still are.

XOXOXO

May God continue to heal
and strengthen your body, mind
& your quintessential spirit!
With all Our love " 🐛 "
Mm & Wil

Every morning & afternoon,
rain or shine, I see you
with a smile on your face
at the crosswalk. You wave
to every car & smile. I heard
that you are undergoing treatments
and I pray for a speedy
recovery. My husband had
cancer 8 years ago, so I know
how amazing it is for you.
to do what you do. Thank-you
for putting a smile on my
face every day.

Crystal Steward
(Kai's Mom)

thank you

Every day, may you
learn more and more
about your own strength,
lean more and more
upon your remarkable courage.

Nikki,
Every update from you is
inspiring! To see that you
can overcome Anything handed
to you is an example of
how resiliant we all should be!

Love You!

Jayce

Love & Hugs to,
Annie, Marcos, & Caesar

2/7/14

Nikki

I'm thinking feel-betterish thoughts
just as fast as I can.

❋

"If ever there is tomorrow when
we're not together there is
something you must always
remember. You are braver than
you believe, stronger than you
seem and smarter than you
think. But the most important
thing is, even if we're apart, I'll
always be with you." - Winnie
the Pooh 😊   Love Always
Mom & Wil

Nicole,
Thank you for all you have done this school year! I am going to greatly miss you next year! Take care of yourself! God Bless You! :)

It was such a kind and thoughtful, extra-special thing to do.

Love,
Jenn Smith

Nicole,
You are dealing with so much and handling things. Do well. You are an inspiration to everyone. I am praying for you and cheering you on. Love you much.

You meaN So MuCH to So maNy wHo hope you FeEl BetTeR EacH Day.

Love
Daliah
Danielle

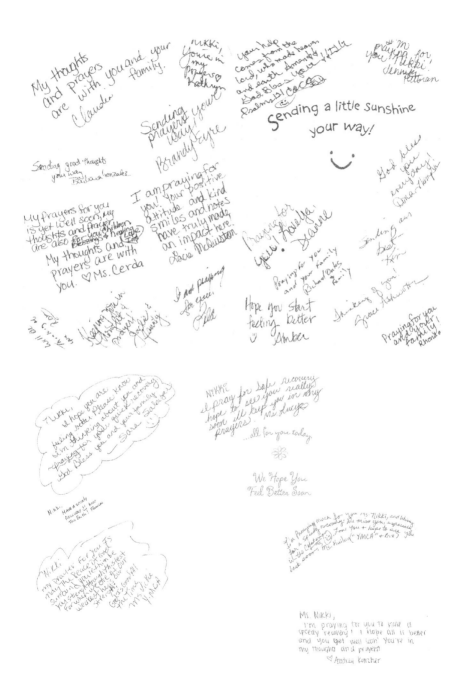

Dear Nikki,
I just wanted to let you know I was thinking about you. Please know you have been in my thoughts & prayers ever since we heard the news. I will be thinking about you & say extra prayers on the 28th. You're a strong woman & I know you'll kick cancers Butt! Prayers coming your way for a quick & easy recovery. Take it easy as much as possible. I enclosed some quotes that I really like & think you will too.

Warm thoughts
and good wishes
are with you.
Hope you're
feeling much better
very soon.

Love &
prayers, love
and positive
thoughts coming
your way

Love,
Cindy
& Family

Just wanted to say
Hi :) you are always
in our thoughts & prayers.
Hope you are feeling a
little better. Say hi to
your beautiful kids for me.
Keep smiling :)

...BUT YOU'RE
TOUGHER!

Love,
Cindy

"Feed your faith and your
fears will starve to death" –
Unknown

BOOK #2

The Journey Continues

Nicole Alyse Dorman

CONTENTS

Preface.. 75

Chapter 1
Decisions, Decisions.. 76

Chapter 2
Here I Go Again! Surgery Time... 78

Chapter 3
Road To Recovery.. 81

Chapter 4
Back To Work; Again!.. 83

Chapter 5
Tamoxifen Side Effects.. 85

Chapter 6
A Surprise For My Boys.. 87

Chapter 7
Writing Didn't Stop W/ "I Fought Like a Girl and I Won!.......... 89

Chapter 8
Returning Back To Chemotherapy.. 90

Chapter 9
Five Year Cancerversary Trip.. 91

Chapter 10
Thank-You Everyone For Your Support!.. 94

Preface

July 2016 Hello World, It's Nicole Dorman again! I've written another book; # The Journey Continues. Everyone in this world is on a journey. Our life paths can take many directions. We don't always know where our life is headed or who we meet along the way. In my first book "I Fought Like a Girl and I Won!"; I was diagnosed with Stage 2 Invasive Ductal Carcinoma breast cancer! The news of my diagnosis stirred up many questions and emotions. I had to make many quick decisions in a small amount of time.

The decisions that I made for my breast cancer treatment were thought out very carefully. My three children were my main reason for not giving up hope! My other reasons were my family, friends, also to see where I will be in life 5-10 years from now! The famous saying "The Journey of 1,000 miles begins with the first step" is very true! The journey of my breast cancer free life began with a right mastectomy, four months of chemotherapy treatments, and 30 radiation treatments. These steps were necessary, along with many prayers to having a second chance in life.

The Journey Continues" will go into the next chapter of my remission life. Part of my journey was very difficult to accept the fact that Anastazija (my daughter who illustrated "I fought Like a Girl and I Won!") wanted to go live with her dad. She moved from Texas to South Carolina on June 6, 2015. It broke my heart to see her move, but I couldn't force her to stay. In life we all need to make decisions and learn from the choices (good and bad) that we make. I didn't know that it would be 18 months before Marcos, Caesar, and I would see Anastazija again. (We surprised her for Christmas of 2016 (December 27, 2016) our road trip from Killeen Texas to South Carolina was 16.5 hours!!! Many thanks to my family, friends, fans, FB followers, IG, Linked In followers for keeping up with my updates.

1.Decisions, Decisions

On July 10, 2014, I had received a call from my oncologist that my CAT scan results were in and there were no signs of cancer in my body! It was a very joyous day, and I wanted that happiness to continue for years to come. Even though my oncologist had cleared me of cancer, I wanted to do more to have a better peace of mind. There were options that I had to think about. In life you always have options! In June 2014 I had the first of several consultations for reconstruction surgery. I initially had a consultation in March 2014 with a plastic surgeon. He asked me what I wanted to do about my left breast. I really needed to think about this question, but I had plenty of time to think it over.

On January 6, 2015 I had a mammogram done on my left breast. The results had come back clear, but who is to say that in five years I would still be healthy? I had a few months to think about keeping my left breast of having a left mastectomy. I was explained in detail my reconstructive options. 1) I could have a silicone implant on the right side, but over time the implant can burst. I would have to come in weekly after having surgery to have tissue ex panders put in to stretch out my skin. This would need to be done to accommodate the implant size I desired. If I chose the silicone implant route, my right breast would look different and not be the same size as my left breast. *News Flash* I was already in that situation after having a right mastectomy! 2) I could choose to not have the surgery and keep wearing a prosthesis. 3) Final option would be to have a procedure called a DIEP Flap. This surgery uses skin and tissue from your back, buttocks, or stomach. This is a lengthy 10-12 hours, complicated procedure with many risks. The surgeon uses a microscope during the surgery to ensure the tissues, and blood vessels are connected properly. The patient is cut hip to hip resulting in a tummy tuck, and re positioning of the belly button! Recovery time is 6-8 weeks with a minimum of 4-5 days in the hospital. There are many risks with this procedure including necrosis (tissue death). In short that means that the surgery wasn't effective! In the event that would happen, then an immediate alternate plan would need to take place. When my appointment was over at the Scott & White Cosmetic Surgery Center in Temple Texas, I felt overloaded with information! In the weeks following my appointment, I received a call from Scott & White informing me of my next consultation appointment date. My June 2015 appointment quickly approached. I had weighed the pro's and con's countless times deciding to have the surgery or not. It is my body and my decision on what I want to do. I started remembering my cancer journey and what I had already been through. Right mastectomy, port-a-cath placement surgery, chemotherapy, and radiation treatments. I thought to myself "haven't I been through enough?" I thought to myself again "what if I developed breast cancer again in my left breast in a few years?" That was a very scary thought! I didn't want to go through that again! I wanted to have peace of mind, and not to worry about the possibility of discovering another lump. One very important thing my oncologist had warned me about was: if my breast cancer returned it would be much worse! My chances of survival would be at a lower percentage rate. I did not want to take that risk at all! Now, back to my appointment with the plastic surgeon; I was asked if I had made a final decision on what I was going to do. I told the plastic surgeon I had made my mind up and have decided to have the DIEP flap, left mastectomy, and to have both breasts reconstructed! The next step was to wait for the surgery scheduler to call me with a surgery date. I requested for the same Temple VA surgeon who performed my right mastectomy in January 2014. I was hoping to have the surgery in June or early July because of my work schedule with Killeen Independent School District. I was given a July 29, 2015 surgery date, but not given a report time just yet. On July 14, 2015 I had a few pre-op appointments, and an appointment with the admissions department. When I had my right mastectomy in January 2014, the procedure was performed at the Temple VA Hospital. This time I would be having the surgery at Scott & White Hospital because I was having the DIEP Flap and the Temple VA Hospital didn't do that procedure there. Since I was a referral from the VA Hospital, they would be paying for the expensive surgery and hospital stay. The admissions clerk had to verify with the Temple VA Hospital that they had referred me to Scott & White. Once all my information was verified I was able to leave my appointment in confidence. I went home and began writing my to do list for the next two weeks! There were so many things to think of and plan to do before my "Big Day"! I thought to myself,who was going to help watch my boys for a few days while I was in the hospital? I had a short list of people to ask, because my friends had families of their own and their own lives going on. It was short notice; but I asked my mother in Pennsylvania to come help me out with my boys while I was recovering.

2. Here I Go Again! Surgery Time

I only had two weeks to go until my big day, and I had a lot to take care of! I asked a friend of mine if she could watch my boys while I was at Scott & White. Kristine asked her husband Mac if it was okay for my boys Marcos and Caesar to stay with them from Tuesday July 28, 2015 until Sunday August 2, 2015. Kristine and Mac have two boys around the same ages as my two boys. Marcos and Caesar were thrilled when I told them that they were staying with Ms. Kristine, Mr. Mac and their boys for a few days! I packed enough food, clothes, and toys for the boys to last their stay.

My friend Frances drove me to Scott & White early Wednesday morning. My report time was at 6:00 am, once I was checked in I had to wait in the waiting area with my buzzer. Once I saw my name appear on the screen my buzzer went off and I knew that it was close to showtime! The butterflies in my stomach began to flutter as I was shown what room to go to. I changed into a gown, foot totes, and a hair cover. Shortly after I was changed the surgeon had come into the room to draw on me with a red maker. My surgeon marked my stomach so he and his team would know how much skin and tissue to remove. 7:30 am quickly approached as I had my I.V. put in my left arm and was taken to the OR. My anxiety set in as I looked up at the ceiling while being wheeled down the long hallway! There was no turning back to have this ten-hour procedure. It's funny (weird not ha ha) how life turns out to be years ago, I would have never imagined myself having plastic surgery. I'm not against it at all; I just never saw me as a candidate to have it done. Breast cancer changed my life a lot; it put so many things in perspective.not. I don't stress on the small things in life. I survived cancer and everything else is a walk in the park! I never considered writing until I was going through breast cancer treatments.

I didn't know how much my first book "I Fought Like a Girl and I Won!" had helped so many other breast cancer patients! It really makes me feel good to be able to help other people get through their own cancer battles, and journeys! I have had so many people be so loving and supportive to me while I was going through my battle, now it's my turn to pay it forward. Now back to my story! Once I was wheeled into the OR everything began to look real blurry! I began to get extremely nervous once I looked around the OR room and saw my medical team, and tons of surgical tools. I felt my heart beating faster! It wasn't long before I was completely asleep. I slowly woke up around 6:30pm in the recovery room. I was groggy but relieved to have had another successfully surgery! I remember that my throat was as dry as the Sahara Desert! I was only allowed to chew ice chips! I hadn't eaten anything since before 11pm the night before, I was STARVING! I had spent two hours in the recovery room, and at 9pm I was ready to go to my room. I was in a lot of pain and was ready to take my medicine! Rest was not on my schedule for that first night, and I'll tell you why! When I arrived in my room there was a maintenance worker repairing a wall switch behind my bed! I couldn't get into a comfortable sleeping position! The type of surgery I had really restricted my movements and sleeping positions. I was only allowed to sleep in the sitting up position. I don't know about you; but I'm a side and stomach sleeper.

I had a tummy tuck which meant I was cut from hip to hip or 12 inches; I wasn't able to lie flat; nor did I even want to think about laying flat! The pain was unbearable! Considering the type of surgeries I had, (port-a-cath removal, left mastectomy, DIEP Flap) I thought I would have been prescribed some stronger pain medicine. Wrong.....Tylenol 3 is what is was given in the hospital. I had stronger pain medicine when I had my first surgery my right mastectomy in January 2014. Continuing on.... I pressed the call buttonnear my bed to have a nurse come adjust my bed so I could be more comfortable. I didn't have towait long for a nurse to come to my room, but she was not paying attention to me when I said stop moving my head board down! I had excruciating pain, I felt like I was being pulled apart!I had to wear a catheter because I couldn't get out of bed, let alone walk the short distance to my bathroom.

I wore leg massagers round the clock in bed to prevent blood clots. I had to be unhooked from everything every time I got out of the hospital bed. The second day after my surgery I slowly, and I mean s-l-o-w-l-y got out of the bed using a walker. I told my nurses that I didn't want any help. I didn't want to have to stay in the hospital any longer than I had to! My friends and family know that I am a very independent women and a fighter! I didn't want to be dependent on anyone during my recovery time, or feel like I was being a burden. As I walked around the hallway I looked down at my legs and they were swollen like pork sausages! I was on a 24 hour liquid diet following my surgery.

I was so determined to get back on my feet literally for a shorter recovery time. I had read that the recovery time for the type of surgery I had was 6-8 weeks! I had my TRAM flaps monitored by a Doppler system every hour for the first 24 hours. This was necessary to make sure the new tissue (my reconstructed breast) was getting enough blood flow! Necrosis (tissue death) is a common risk with this kind of surgery.

I was at low risk for necrosis because I was under 40, I had no major health issues, and I am a non-smoker. In the event that necrosis happened, then an alternate plan would have had to be put into action.

3. *Road To Recovery*

Two weeks before my surgery, I had been trying to figure out a way for my mom to come to visit me in Killeen, Texas. I wanted my mom to help with her grandsons Marcos, and Caesar when I got discharged from the hospital. My finances were very tight, but I had prayed that everything would work out in the end. I searched for cheap flights on Spirit.com and I found one! I called my mother to tell her that I found a reasonable flight leaving Baltimore, and arriving in Dallas/Fort Worth nonstop on Saturday August 1, 2015. I looked at the flights and began working on details on where my mom would stay for her visit. My Choice Rewards points came in handy for 2 free nights! Everything was working out great so far; I had to figure out how to get my mom from the DFW International airport to Killeen. I was already going to be in the hospital because my surgery date was July 29, 2015. I did a group message on my IPhone to ask some friends and my cousin Joyce if anyone was available to pick up my mother. I had received numerous texts that people had plans; that was expected since I did ask last minute. It was summertime and a Saturday; of course people had plans! A couple hours after sending the text, my cousin Joyce responded back that she would be able to pick up Aunt Pam (my mom). I was so ecstatic that everything was working out! I texted my mom telling her that her niece Joyce would be picking her up. I asked my cousin to call my mom so they could make plans. My mom had called me to let me know that on the way back to Killeen from Dallas she was going to visit her sister (my Aunt Niki) in Belton. I asked my mom if she would visit me at the Scott & White Hospital in Temple, Texas. I didn't know how many day I was going to be admitted in the hospital, I knew it would be a minimum of 4 days. I called my friend Kristine to inform her that my mom would be picking up her grandsons on Sunday August 2, 2015. I gave my mother's number to Kristine so they could coordinate plans. With one less thing to worry about, I was able to go into the hospital and not have any extra stress. Saturday night August 1, 2015 my mother, cousin Joyce and her two daughters Jessica, and Jasmine (my other cousins), my Aunt Dee-Dee all came to visit me in the hospital. I was so happy to see everyone, and to know that my mother had arrived safely.

Fast forwarding, I had my surgery as you read in chapter 2. Sunday August 2, 2015 came and at 7:30am the doctor mad his morning rounds. My vitals were taken, and I was told that I was being discharged! I was happy, but also I was still in a great amount of pain. I hadn't had a bowel movement, that used to be a requirement for a patient to do before being discharged. I started making phone calls to find out who was able to pick me up from the hospital. I had everything figured out except how I was getting to the hotel to be with my mother and boys! I called my friend Frances and asked her if she could pick me up. I was finally getting discharged at noon. I had my discharge paperwork and future follow up appointments. I had 2 prescriptions to pick up at the pharmacy. I was swollen, in extreme pain and I had 4 JP drains (Jackson Pratt drains) attached to me! I felt like a marionette puppet more now that when I had my right mastectomy! Having tubes stitched to my sides was not fun! I had limited mobility, but luckily I had all 4 Jackson Pratt drains removed within 3 weeks of my surgery.

I spent 4 weeks recovering and healing from the reconstructive surgery. The first day of school was August 24, 2015. It was my last week off before returning to work as a crossing guard. I have had my weekly follow-up visits to see my nurse and plastic surgeon. I remember my first post surgery visit I was in pain all over! The worst pain I've experienced was when my left hip JP drain was clogged 4 days after surgery. The tube was clogged so bad, it had to be pulled out; that was easier said than done! Just thinking about having the JP drain tube pulled out made me wench before it actually happened. Pulling out the JP tube consisted of the nurse telling me to hold my breath and her pulling the tube out. This is no short tube;in fact I still have no idea how the tube goes into the body. I was sore but also relieved that the tube and drain were removed from my left hip!

I kept all my Facebook friends and family informed on my healing progress. I was driving 1 week after my surgery date. I didn't want to rely on anyone to drive me to my appointments, or anywhere else I needed to go. I also didn't want to be a burden to anyone. If I was driving somewhere, I simply didn't take my pain medication until my bedtime. My Aunt Dee-Dee did take me to a few follow-up appointments after my surgery. I had several appointments after my first two weeks of recovery; I was able to drive comfortably. A very special thanks goes out to my friend Deshonn A.; who used to be a nurse, and she is a fellow Military Veteran. Deshonn was able to give me extra bandages, gauze, and medical tape. She taught me how to pack my stomach properly, and let me borrow a wedge pillow which made sleeping on my back much more comfortable. When I was discharged from Scott & White, I was given limited medical supplies, so it was truly a blessing for Deshonn to give me medical advice and help.

4. Back To Work; Again!

I was told that the average healing time for the left mastectomy and reconstruction of both breasts using the DIEP Flap was going to be 6-8 weeks! I am NOT the average healer/patient!! My first day back to work was Monday August 31, 2015. I was happy to be back at work as a crossing guard, crossing the students again for the 2015/2016 school year. I hadmissed the first week of school which is always a hectic, but an exciting time for parents and staff alike.

I had just finished my am. crossing shift when my Aunt Dee called me at 9:44am to inform me that my Aunt Niki had died at 8:40 am at Scott +White Hospital in Temple Texas. Scott+White Hospital is the same hospital I was at having surgery, less than a month prior. I was devastated to say the least that my aunt had passed away one day before her birthday. My mom had visited my Aunt Niki while she was visiting me in early August. My mom thanked me for bugging her to come visit me to help out with the boys, otherwise she wouldn't have seen her sister one last time. In life we cannot go back in the past, but I wish that I had made more time to go visit her when she still alive. A life lesson for everyone is to not dwell in the past, but to focus and to be positive for the future.

At the school I worked at MVE, I had parents who hadn't seen me in a while ask me if I was still a crossing guard. I had explained to them the I had reconstruction surgery and was off for four weeks for recovery. The first week back to work I kept reminding myself to take it easy and to not lift over 15 lbs! My stomach incisions were not completely healed. I had to go see my nurse weekly to try different way to help my incision heal fast.

I went to see my nurse up until the middle of September, 2015. My incisions finally healed completely, and I was so relieved to not have to wear bandages, gauze, and medical tape!

Getting back into my daily routine was not easy. I had to get up earlier because I was not moving around at my normal speed. I had to make sure the kids were up on time, dressed for school, brush their teeth and hair, and ready to walk out the door by 6:30 am! The weeks went on and I was back to regular self in no time. Some words of advice for quick healing from surgery are; eating a lot of protein, drinking plenty of water, moving around at your own pace, don't rush around for anyone!

5. *Tamoxifen Side Effects*

In September, 2015 it was a year that I've been taking tamoxifen. I've been very blessed to have had very few side effects with this prescription drug. I did have a scare in November 2014, two months after I had been taking tamoxifen. I had driven myself to the Temple VA ER. I had chest pains continuously for 4 hours. The ER nurse had said that I might have had a PE (pulmonary embolism) a blood clot in my lung! Are you kidding me?! What the heck was I going to do if I had a blood clot in my lung? I didn't want to jump to conclusions but I was getting worried. I had a chest x-ray that ruled out that I didn't have a PE. I had a big sigh of relief, and I was given pain medication. I had to follow up with my primary care doctor within a few days of being released from the ER. When I had my next appointment with my oncologist, I asked her if it was really necessary for me to keep taking the tamoxifen. My oncologist explainedto me that it is really important to continue taking the tamoxifen. Although I have had a right mastectomy, chemotherapy, and radiation therapy, the tamoxifen was in effect to make sure that there are no more cancer cells in my body.

Originally I was seeing my oncologist every 3 months, but I have doing so well my doctor recommended me to come see her every 5 months. To me that was excellent news, because I would have less appointments, and I wouldn't have to drive 45 minutes one way to be seen. I found out from my oncologist that I'm allowed to have my eyes examined by the VA optometrist once a year. Another side effect of tamoxifen is that it may change your vision. I agreed for my doctor to put in a consultation for me to have my eyes examined. I was called with an appointment date and time for February 23, 2016 @ 10:30am. I received an appointment reminder along with a heads up that I may have my eyes dilated at the appointment. I asked a friend of mine if she would be able to take me to my appointment. This was my first time havingmy eyes dilated since I was a 10 year old girl. I remember how blurry my vision was and that it took a long time for my vision to return to normal.

I was seen promptly at my eye appointment, and the total exam time was 1 ½ hours. My optometrist had a concern and asked me if anyone in my family had glaucoma. I told her not to my knowledge. My right optic nerve is larger than my left. I had always thought that glaucoma was an eye disease that senior citizens got not people under 40 years old! I did my research and I did find out that being part African-American and close to 40, had put me at risk. I waited for a separate appointment date for my glaucoma test. In March 2016, I received my prescriptions glasses arrived by mail. It felt weird wearing glasses again after not wearing them for 8 years. InMarch I also had my glaucoma test, my results were normal. I continue to go to yearly eye exams and have glaucoma tests while I'm still taking tamoxifen. There are many other side effects to taking tamoxifen, but I haven't experienced anything else. I continue to count my blessings!

6. A Surprise For My Two Boys!

When I was first diagnosed with breast cancer, I had researched many organizations that offered assistance. One organization; 3 Little Birds For Life, grants wishes for adults who have cancer and for adults who are in remission. Shortly after completing the paperwork, I was contacted by a wish granter. I was told that each individual who had a wish granted had a budget. That made made sense because there were other people who were waiting to have their wishes granted too! Originally, I wanted to go to Disney world in Orlando, Florida with my sons, but I had to be realistic, cost effective, and not selfish. I had lived in Texas since February 17, 2001 and I have been to San Antonio,Dallas, Houston, Austin, many times. I thought for a long time about where the perfect family vacation would be and what dates would be good for my schedule. I thought about what my boys really liked Lego's, and Star Wars; I had the perfect vacation destination........... Lego land in Carlsbad, California. Carlsbad, California is 2 hours from Los Angeles; I had never been to Los Angeles so Lego land was definitely a winner! I had let 3 Little Birds For Life know in January 2016 what my "wish" decision was. The dates that I had picked were March 13-17, 2016 (spring break) for our surprise family vacay! It was hard to keep the trip a surprise from my boys for 3 months, but I did it! 3 Little Birds For Life arranged for our flights from Dallas (DFW) to Los Angeles (LAX) on Spirit Airlines. Arrangements were also made for entrance into Lego land and the Aquarium. This surprise trip was a true blessing and I am grateful for the employees who are involved with granting wishes, volunteers who donate their time, and people who donate money to this organization! I was responsible for paying for our hotel, meals, and souvenirs.

My boys and I enjoyed Lego land, Venice Beach, Hollywood Blvd, meeting Spider-man, Madam Tussaud's Wax Museum and taking Amtrak from Union Station to Oceanside, Ca. From Oceanside, Ca we took a 20 minute taxi ride to Carlsbad, Ca. We went to eat at Sweetie Pies; TJ's location in NOHO. I found out after taking taxi's for the first two days of our vacation, that it was cheaper to order an Uber. I had such a fantastic experience with the Uber drivers in Los Angeles I was inspired to become an Uber and Lyft driver in Killeen, Texas! Seeing Los Angeles traffic in person is much different that what you see in the movies! I'm so glad that we flew and didn't drive! Speaking of flying........ LAX is not what I pictured it to be either; there was so much construction, and I didn't see one celebrity!

The trip to Los Angeles Ca was a well deserved vacation for my boys and I. Going to Lego land was the perfect break for everyone. My boys had handled the diagnosis of my breast cancer at age 5, and 8 years old like champions! I was so happy to take them on a vacation memory of a lifetime! I was blessed that I was in remission to appreciate the trip with them! We definitely want to return to Los Angeles in the near future; maybe we will visit Knots Berry Farms!

It is very important to make family memories with your children while they are young, because they grow up in a blink of an eye! You don't have to spend a lot of money and you definitely don't have to have a lot of money to have quality time with the people who matter the most in your life.

7. Writing Didn't Stop w/ I Fought Like a Girl and I Won!

It has been over 3 years since I started writing "#The Journey Continues." I took a break from writing it to start a completely different project......... a movie script! I had the mind framethat I wrote a book, why not write a movie script?! I took my writing skills to the next level and I began writing "The Wrong Recipient". In July 2016. It is a modern day version of Ransom meets Fugitive with a twist. Are you interested in a preview of what "The Wrong Recipient" is about? Well here you go...... Evelyn Myers is a young attractive law student who attends New York Law in Manhattan. She thinks her life is dull and unpredictable attending school, and stripping on the weekends. Prison escapee Clyde Castro kills his friend over a large sum of money. His greed makes him hunt down his victims daughter Evelin Mayers; a New York Law professor. With no address for Professor Evelin Mayers, Clyde delivers a letter at the admissionsoffice. When student Evelyn Myers receives the letter by mistake she is scared for her life. In a state of panic Evelyn is running for her life in the Big Apple. Chaos and murder happen when you mistake someone's identity in "The Wrong Recipient"!

I have my movie script registered with The Writer's Guild America West (WGAW). I am optimistic about my movies script and I have had some positive feedback from people whom I shared my script with. I am thinking for my next project to change the script to an action/thriller book! So please stay tuned!

When I was in school, I never thought of becoming an author. I didn't even consider writing until after I was finished with my radiation, and chemotherapy. I have always enjoyed writing; but I became more passionate about it when I wrote "I Fought Like a Girl and I Won!"

If your passionate for something you are good at; pursue your dreams. Don't let other people deter you from your dreams, goals, and ambitions. You won't know who you help out, and inspire by continuing to do the things you already enjoy!

8. Back To The Chemotherapy Room

June 25, 2014 was my final chemotherapy treatment at the Temple VA. Although I pass the chemotherapy treatment room when I have appointments with my oncologist, I didn't think that I would be going back there. At my appointments with my oncologist I always discuss what the next steps of my treatment are. On October 23, 2017 I had my first infusion of Lupron. What is Lupron you ask? Lupron is a shot primarily for men who have prostate cancer, women who have endometriosis, and for children who are starting puberty too soon! I obviously don't fit into any of those categories, so why am I getting the shot? Good question; and I'll tell you why! Since I have a family history of breast cancer and my breast cancer was brought on by my hormone receptors, my oncologist advised that Lupron will be additional protection. I have to get the shot every 3 months, and I rotate the arm that I receive the infusion in. I go to the chemotherapy room to receive the shot and there are all new nurses in there since my last chemotherapy treatment. I have never had a problem receiving shots before, but the needle for the Lupron injection is about 2 or more inches long! A few hours after receiving the injection my right arm was extremely sore.

I was advised not to massage my arm; however I could apply cold/warm compresses! 3 months medication sitting on your arm is not a pleasant feeling, but it also isn't the worst thing in the world! It was like a big knot was in my arm and the pain lasted for 3 days after the injection! I'm no wimp, however I ended up going to the VA ER and I was prescribed antibiotics. I had a high fever, and I had some other side effects that I was concerned about. Remember, when in doubt; get it checked out! I was concerned about the possibility of being allergic! I wandered if I was going to get these side effects every 3 months? Surely not! I had learned to be patient and let my body get used to this strong medicine. Lupron has a long list of side effects, mainly for men who are taking it. For me I have gained around 70 pounds, and I haven't had a menstrual cycle because my ovaries are in suppression. The hot flashes I have are horrible sometimes!

9. Five Year Cancerversary Trip!

I always get the chills when I think about my breast cancer diagnosis date and my remission date. Why do you ask? It's because both dates contain same numbers. 107 is date that I will never forget because that's my diagnosis date. My remission date is 710, and both dates are special to me.

In May 2019, I started to do some planning of what I wanted to do to celebrate 5 years of being cancer free! I hadn't done anything special the previous years; but I know other cancer survivors do something special and memorable to celebrate their 5 year anniversary! I wanted to include my boys in my celebration plans; after all the fighting, surgeries and treatments I underwent for all for my children! I didn't have a lot of money saved up, but my son's and I went on a 7,265 mile road trip! Where did we go? It's more like where didn't we go? Our vacation started June 25, 2019 (last chemotherapy anniversary) my kids and I loaded up our 2008 Cadillac SRX and drove 30 hours from Killeen, Texas to The Dalles, Oregon! My boys have grandparents on their father's side of the family that live in Oregon. While we kept in touch with grandma V, grandpa M, and great-grandma D over the years; it's been over 10 years since the boys have seen them in person! Surviving breast cancer has made me realize so many things. Everyone is getting older, and the main reason that has kept my kids from visiting their grand parent's in Oregon more was my lack of money. Well I'm tired of using 'lack of money" as an excuse for doing things and living life! Everyday is really a gift, and while we cannot go back in the past memories do last a lifetime! We spent 3 weeks in Oregon and had a blast! As a family we took a 4 mile round trip hike in Tamanawas Falls. It was 2 miles to get the to most beautiful waterfall we had ever seen! We learned that Oregon is famous for it's cherry orchards , and wine vineyards! I've found out cherries have many health benefits if you eat them daily. We visited the Oregon Veterans Home in The Dalles. The boys got to see their aunt and uncle's 80 74acre cherry orchard, and pick cherries! We got to see snow on Mount Hood in June!!! We visited Timberline Lodge where they filmed the movie "The Shining"! Fourth of July was the best! The Pacific Ocean was cold! Living in Texas we are used to 100+ degree' weather! We got a break from the heat, and the weather was 65 degrees during the day and in the 40's at night. The boys and their grandpa M put the tent up, and my oldest son chopped firewood with an axe!

We spent 5 days camping near Long Beach Washington on the Washington Peninsula! On the beach we had front row seats to a 3 hour firework spectacular show! On the way back to Oregon from the beach, while we were already in Astoria we went past the iconic "Goonies" house! You cannot put a price tag on making found memories with loved ones and your children!

At the end of our Oregon trip we came back to Killeen TX for a few days to unpack, unload the car, and repack for Pennsylvania. 2019 summer of memories was in full effect! I had a 22 hour drive ahead of me to go to Harrisburg, PA, but being the road warrior that I am I didn't mind the drive at all. Seeing my mom, step father, brother, and my sister-in-law was great! I haven't been to Harrisburg, PA in over 2 years to visit my mom, and step-father. For those of you who don't know, you have to visit Hershey which is 15 minutes from Harrisburg. Hershey is nicknamed "Chocolate town USA" there is Hershey Park, with a water park and Zoo America inside. There is Chocolate World which is an all day attraction itself to include an amazing educational ride to see first hand how Hershey chocolate is made! You also will get to take a Trolley Works tour to drive through the town of Hershey, and also tour parts of the Milton Hershey School which I am proud to say I am an alumni of. I attended the Milton Hershey School from 1989-1996. Since my graduation, my brother and 2 cousins have attended! I am blessed to be part of the vision that Milton and Catherine Hershey visioned a long time ago! I have always been thankful to my mother for giving me the gift of better opportunities and having a better education. I don't know where I would be today if I didn't attend the Milton Hershey School! ***Thanks Mom, I love you!!!***

10. Thank-You Everyone For Your Support!!

This final chapter is a specially dedicated for everyone who has been apart of my breast cancer journey from my diagnosis on January 7, 2014 up until now! I couldn't have survived my journey alone.

The reason I wrote "I Fought Like a Girl and I Won!" was to share my breast cancer journey as a working single mother of 3 young children. I am not famous, just extraordinary Nicole Dorman who wanted to share with other people. People who know someone who is being newly diagnosed with any type of cancer, a spouse, sibling, grandparent, of someone who has cancer, or YOU may be that person who has cancer and needs help, advise, inspiration. I want to encourage other young adults, women, men who have battled their own cancer journey to write a journal or perhaps write a book like I did! Yes! It took courage to tell my story and I've had a few personal friends turn to me for advice after they have been diagnosed with Cancer! I have found out in life that people are blindsided to important issues in life UNTIL they or a loved one is affected!

Please keep in contact with me by visiting my website http://ifoughtlikeagirlandiwon.home.blog also please like my Face Book page "I Fought Like a Girl and I Won!" and on Instagram "I Fought Like a Girl and I Won!" I also welcome emails from everyone who has questions or concerns, or if you just feel alone and need uplifting! Please feel free to reach me at nicoledorman1979@icloud.com.

If you have an interest in wanting to write a book, and don't know where to begin with the writing process don't be afraid to contact me for help! I will never be too busy to listen to you and I'm not asking for any money from you!

God Bless Everyone, and remember that if something doesn't feel right about your health, go to your doctor and get checked. Don't second guess; early detection is the best!

CERTIFICATE OF COMPLETION

PRESENTED TO

Nicole Dorman

for completing the prescribed course of Radiation Therapy with the highest degree of Courage, Determination and Good Nature. We appreciate the confidence placed in us and the opportunity to serve you!

Given this 10th day of September 2014

Therapist

Physician

Therapist

Made in the USA
Las Vegas, NV
14 January 2022

41433012R00057